TRADITION TODAY

CONTINUITY IN ARCHITECTURE & SOCIETY

WITPRESS

WIT Press publishes leading books in Science and Technology.
Visit our website for the current list of titles.
www.witpress.com

WITeLibrary

Home of the Transactions of the Wessex Institute, the WIT electronic-library
provides the international scientific community with immediate and permanent
access to individual papers presented at WIT conferences.
Visit the WIT eLibrary at http://library.witpress.com

TRADITION TODAY

CONTINUITY IN ARCHITECTURE & SOCIETY

Edited by

Robert Adam & Matthew Hardy

I · N · T · B · A · U
PATRON: HIS ROYAL HIGHNESS THE PRINCE OF WALES

WITPRESS **Southampton, Boston**

Edited by:

Robert Adam
Robert Adam Architects, UK

Matthew Hardy
International Network for Traditional Building, Architecture & Urbanism, UK

Cover typography by Richard Kindersley.

INTBAU is a worldwide organisation dedicated to the support of traditional building, the maintenance of local character and the creation of better places to live. We are creating an active network of individuals and institutions who design, make, maintain, study or enjoy traditional building, architecture and places. Read more about INTBAU at http://www.intbau.org/.

Published by

WIT Press
Ashurst Lodge, Ashurst, Southampton, SO40 7AA, UK
Tel: 44 (0) 238 029 3223; Fax: 44 (0) 238 029 2853
E-Mail: witpress@witpress.com
http://www.witpress.com

For USA, Canada and Mexico

WIT Press
25 Bridge Street, Billerica, MA 01821, USA
Tel: 978 667 5841; Fax: 978 667 7582
E-Mail: infousa@witpress.com
http://www.witpress.com

British Library Cataloguing-in-Publication Data

A Catalogue record for this book is available from the British Library

ISBN: 978-1-84564-066-8

Library of Congress Catalog Card Number: 2007943643

The texts of the papers in this volume were set individually by the authors or under their supervision.

CONTENTS

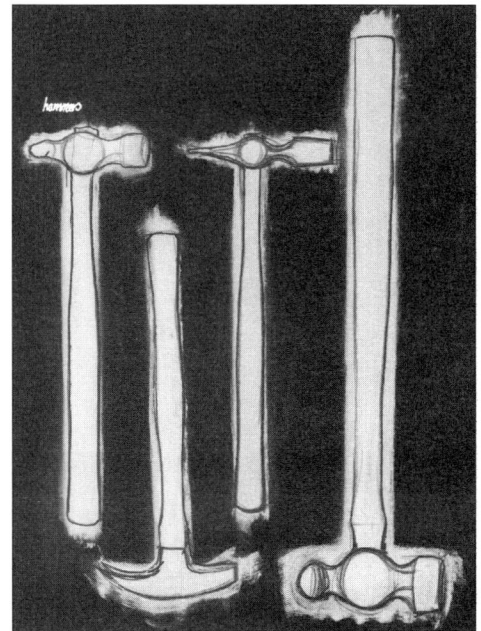

Malca Schotten: Blacksmith tools-hammers, 2005, pastel and charcoal on painted paper, 70cm x 100cm. Reproduced by permission of the artist.

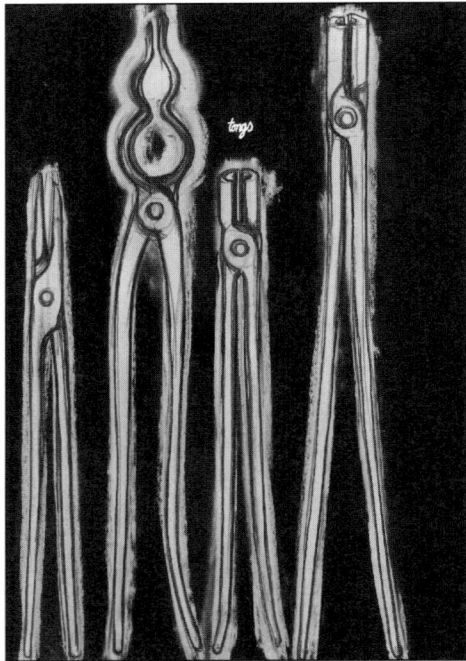

Malca Schotten: Blacksmith tools-tongs,
2005, pastel and charcoal on painted paper,
70cm x 100cm. Reproduced by
permission of the artist.

I am extremely pleased that the International Network for Traditional Building, Architecture and Urbanism (I.N.T.B.A.U.) appears to have caught the imagination and support of so many people already, and I hope, too, that with the association and support of my own Foundation for the Built Environment, the network will develop in the months ahead.

Tradition, I am afraid to say, is a term that has been much maligned and misunderstood in recent years. We live in a world that has become so pre-occupied with change and innovation, that we can all too easily forget how crucial traditions are in handing on the immense richness of human knowledge, wisdom and skill. Instead of acknowledging, respecting and *integrating* our traditions with innovatory science and art, the last century has witnessed a rather dismal tendency to discard our inheritance. All too often the baby has been thrown out with the bath water, with tradition being consigned to the museums or the history books. This tendency has applied across many, perhaps most, fields of human endeavour, and I have tried in recent years to sponsor some initiatives that are trying to forge an alternative. For instance, my Foundation for the Built Environment promotes the integration of traditional techniques in urban planning and design, the fine and applied arts, to support more sustainable and humane living environments; my Foundation for Integrated Health is making similar attempts to bring together the best in traditional medical practice, not as an *alternative* to the orthodox approach, but to integrate with it - combining the best from both traditions; and my efforts to encourage organic agricultural practices also draw heavily from techniques that, until quite recently, appeared to be in danger of disappearing altogether. These examples are not ones that seek to *preserve* traditions as empty gestures, but rather are trying to create the basis for traditions to *live again,* to be practised in the real world and once more help people to *re-connect* with their past, instead of being forever *disconnected* from it. If (and it is, I fear, a very big "if!") we are successful in this approach, then I happen to believe that we will not only discover a more humane and habitable environment, a better way of life, but we will also have a far more likely chance of saving our world's resources for the benefit of future generations.

I am convinced from all of my travels to other countries and cultures, and from all of the people that I meet, both in this country and abroad, that there is a universal human need for places that express a fundamental sense of humanity and harmony. I.N.T.B.A.U.'s network, by connecting traditional craftsmen, designers and others around the world, has become quite a force for keeping these "organic", living traditions alive at a time when they are under more serious threat than at any time in history.

Knowing where we are in our community is all about shared history and the special way we do things – our traditions. These traditions make our past an organic part of our lives, and make the lives we live so much richer. They also, at the same time, give us something precious we can pass on to our children. There is nothing wrong with being "modern" or up-to-date, but the idea that this means we should just cast off all the traditions and roots that give us our place in the world is very damaging indeed, and is clearly causing many problems, whether social, economic or environmental, across the globe.

Traditional building and traditional places have lessons for us all. They are not just the fantasy of some architect or planner who wants to make his or her mark on the world; they have often evolved over centuries to suit the local climate and make best use of local materials – sometimes in ways we do not realize until we try and do something different. Traditional places belong to the communities that live in them; they grow up together and are part of one another. This bond means that the places can change as the community changes, but in a kindly sort of way that does not jar or upset the balance. Traditional places and buildings improve our quality of life. It is no accident that these are the places where most people want to live - including, of course, most of the architects who are first to ridicule traditional architecture!

I am delighted that I.N.T.B.A.U. is going to help to keep these ideas and practices alive and I am very interested to see how we will link ideas about traditions across all kinds of different aspects of society, art and culture.

Subscribers List

The publication of Tradition Today, our first book, was generously supported by the following INTBAU members, listed in order of receipt:

Platinum Subscribers

Mrs Montse Soldevila Casals
Mr & Mrs William and Tanya Frost

Gold Subscribers

Pier Carlo Bontempi
Robert Adam Architects
ROSE Property Group, Australia
Marival
Edward Nash
BLACKBALL International Development, Architecture &
Interior Design

Silver Subscribers

Matthew Hardy
Cyndi Chiao Gadhia
Christine G.H. Franck
Ben Bolgar
Robert T. Cole (Holloway White Allom)
Nicholas Groves-Raines
Alireza Sagharchi RIBA, FRSA
Luke Moloney
Jose Baganha Arquitectos Lda.
C. Giorgetti
Mark Hoare

Arcade in Bath
Photograph courtesy of The Prince's Foundation

Bronze Subscribers

Rupert Pearson
Richard Franklin Sammons
Professor Carrol W. Westfall
Dorin I. Boilă
John Bliss
Peter Kellow
Scott J. Strachan
Tim Bricker
Chief Mrs May Egbunike – Agbakoba
Alvin Holm AIA
Peter Walter
Ferguson & Shamamian Architects
Krier · Kohl · Architekten
Susan Parham
Pittsburgh History & Landmarks Foundation
Kirk Watson
Todd E. Furgason
Jacinta McLynskey
Alan Baxter Associates
Besim S. Hakim FAICP, AIA
Sherban Cantacuzino
Tobias Nöfer
Pim Hienkens
Dr Hubertus J. Michels
Victor Allen
Madison Spencer
Sir Philip Naylor-Leyland Bt
Ibolya Balint

Kim Moreton
Jill Patrick
Aaron M. Helfand
Duncan McCallum McRoberts
Ed Taylor
Jennifer M. Hillier
Robert Patzschke
Dr Debabardhan Upadhyaya
Ricardo Arosemena
Richard Erganian
Alan Lindsay Berry
Philipp Maaß
Urban Planning Institute of Belgrade

TRADITION TODAY
INTRODUCTION

In January 2002, after a two year gestation period, the International Network for Traditional Building, Architecture and Urbanism (INTBAU) was launched. To celebrate the launch, a conference was held to debate the place of tradition in modern society. While INTBAU was specifically concerned with building and urbanism, if tradition was indeed relevant then it must have a place throughout society. The conference is the basis of this book.

In the preparation of the Charter for INTBAU (published on page xi), it became clear that the acceptance or rejection of tradition was a watershed in the design professions and the arts. So powerful was the early-twentieth-century rejection of tradition in the arts by Modernism that the followers of that movement today – the majority of the design professions and formally trained artists – still find the word 'tradition' hard to accept with reference to anything modern.

Any dispassionate social observer, however, would very quickly see that many aspects of our lives would be severely curtailed, if not impossible, without engaging with tradition. Important family and community events such as Christmas, political inaugurations or coronations are nothing more or less than traditions and language itself, that defining background to all culture, relies on the passing on of ideas and practices from the past to the future. It is true that, like aspects of language itself, some traditions fall out of use, that society is changing more rapidly than any other historical period and that this could well accelerate the loss of traditions. At the same time, as society and culture are impossible without traditions, not only will some survive but it is highly likely that new ones are under creation.

It is an important feature of traditions that they adapt and change. So, while change accelerates so should the adaptation of traditions. If we rely on tradition for the transmission of culture, then the adaptation of traditions is a matter of importance to all of us. If change occurs without the transmission of culture, then culture itself dies; culture cannot be created anew every day. The evolutionary nature of tradition is something often ignored by supporters and opponents alike. It is important that history – that which measures our distance from the past – is not confused with tradition – the past living through us.

The papers in this book that discuss these points and many others are a fascinating miscellany. There is something for everyone and contributions range from the practical to the academic. A manufacturer of bricks and an artist craftsman discuss the feeling of continuity with their predecessors and the advent of new technology. A sculptor, two architects and urban designers explain the relevance of tradition in their own work in the face of professional antipathy. A lawyer, a scholar of Islamic architecture and a reader in religious education explore aspects of modern society that continue to be defined by their traditions. A philosopher, an anthropologist and a linguist give academic views of tradition in nature, society and speech. There is also an interesting analysis of the changing role of tradition in gastronomy – a vital but often forgotten medium for cultural transmission. There could have been many more, we had hoped to have a military historian, a painter and a poet. Perhaps these are for a future publication.

Reading these papers can leave no doubt about the continued role and significance of tradition, the passion of those who understand its relevance and the dangers inherent in its denial.

Thanks must be extended to all those that made this possible: the speakers themselves, Matthew Hardy the secretary of INTBAU who organised the conference, Cyndi Chiao who undertook the considerable task of bringing all the papers together, the Princes Foundation for the Built Environment who gave us their conference facilities in London, and last but no means least, His Royal Highness the Prince of Wales who has been our enthusiastic patron and supporter.

Robert Adam

INTBAU Charter

The International Network for Traditional Building, Architecture & Urbanism is an active network of individuals and institutions dedicated to the creation of humane and harmonious buildings and places which respect local traditions.

Traditions allow us to recognise the lessons of history, enrich our lives and offer our inheritance to the future. Local, regional and national traditions provide the opportunity for communities to retain their individuality with the advance of globalisation. Through tradition we can preserve our sense of identity and counteract social alienation. People must have the freedom to maintain their traditions.

Traditional buildings and places maintain a balance with nature and society that has been developed over many generations. They enhance our quality of life and are a proper reflection of modern society. Traditional buildings and places can offer a profound modernity beyond novelty and look forward to a better future.

INTBAU brings together those who design, make, maintain, study or enjoy traditional building, architecture and places. We will gain strength, significance and scholarship by association, action and the dissemination of our principles.

Evelyn Chiao: Old Town of Langzhong, Sichuan Province, China 2005. Reproduced by permission of the artist.

Acknowledgements

Many people have helped with the preparation of this book in the five years it has taken to publish. Special thanks are due to Cyndi Chiao Gadhia, who as INTBAU Registrar nursed the book from a series of conference transcripts to a completed manuscript, and pestered the twelve authors for texts, images and permissions. Thanks are also due to the twelve authors, who kept our project at the front of their minds through the pressures of their busy professional and academic lives. We are grateful to Malca Schotten and Martin Shortis for the use of their images, to The Prince's Drawing School for permission to use images by their students, and to The Prince's Foundation for images from their collection. We are most grateful to His Royal Highness The Prince of Wales for permission to reproduce his message to the conference. Final and most important thanks must go to the subscribers, whose generous donations made the publication possible.

THE
NATURE
of
TRADITION

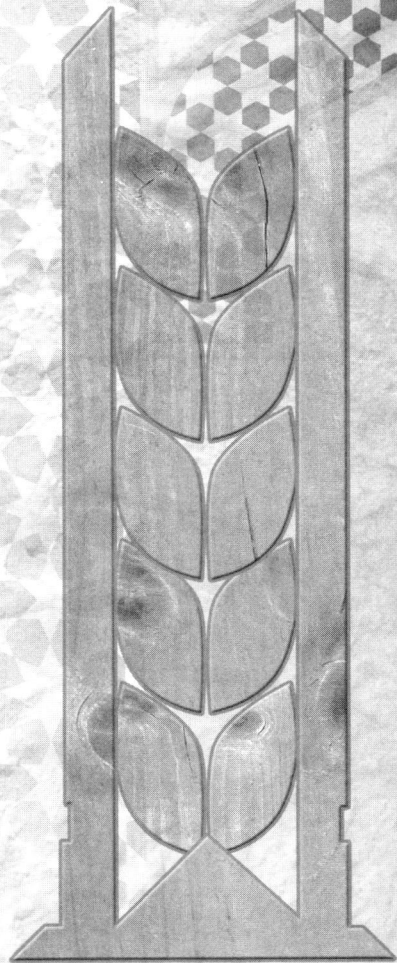

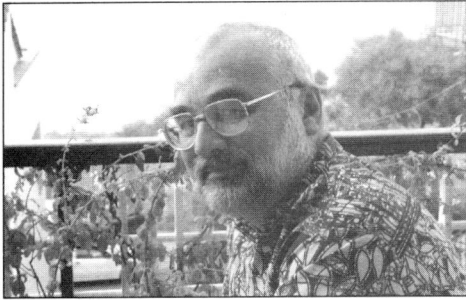

TRANSCENDING TIME: RETHINKING THE INVENTION OF TRADITION

Cesare Poppi

> '... we can see how difficult **Tradition** really is,
> in an abstract or exhortatory or, as so often, ratifying use.'
> Raymond Williams, *Keywords*, London, Fontana (1976)

CESARE POPPI

Born in Bologna in 1953, Cesare Poppi holds a *Laurea in Filosofia* from the University of Bologna and a PhD in Social Anthropology from the University of Cambridge. Having taught the Anthropology of African Art at the University of East Anglia, Norwich, he now teaches Political and Economic Anthropology at the University of Bologna. A dedicated fieldworker, he has lived among the Ladins of the Dolomites and the Vagla and Chakalle of Northwestern Ghana. He has long been interested in issues of cultural identity, ethnicity, tradition and globalization. Amongst his publications, his 'Wider Horizons with larger Details: Subjectivity, Ethnicity and Globalization' (in Alan Scott (ed.) *The Limits of Globalization*, London 1997) is the most relevant to the themes of the present book. He is currently writing a monograph on the *Sigma* secret society of masks in his study on the Strait of Messina.

1. Introduction

Having kindly been asked by the organizers of this Conference to provide a view of tradition from anthropology, I became embarrassingly aware that the discipline which deals with what have been known for the better or worse as 'traditional' societies, has seldom been concerned with reflecting on what precisely the deployment of the term implies.

This applies both to the notion of tradition as an analytical tool and to the concept of tradition as a theoretical construct. The term features abundantly in anthropological literature, but it is used so loosely and casually – and I am aware that many of my colleagues would argue that it cannot but – that leading practitioners have suggested expounding it altogether from the discipline's vocabulary.

It is indeed symptomatic that what was probably the first monograph to address 'tradition' as a viable sociological category, had to wait until the closing decades of the last millennium – 1981 to be precise – to see the daylight. I am referring, of course, to Edward Shils'[1] influential book 'Tradition', first of a series of works that have opened up the debate on the subject of the so-called 'canon' in the last twenty or so years (e.g. Gross [2]; Pelikan [3]).

2. Historical and sociological tradition

Significantly, Shils' work does not spring from Oxbridge, as one might expect from somebody who sees in 'tradition' a central feature of both the social process and sociality itself. He is American and taught sociology at the University of Chicago. Moreover, Shils was the co-translator of Max Weber and Karl Mannheim's works and the major figure, with Talcott Parsons, in the theorization of sociological functionalism. This places him firmly in the modernist mainstream of social theory. At the same time, though, the date of his investigation of tradition situates Shils at that critical junction in the development of modernism where certain assumptions about issues of continuity and cultural value became questioned and finally collapsed.

Shils sees 'tradition' as both an objective cultural phenomenon as well as a concept to understand issues of continuity and change. The failure of modern social thought to reflect on the phenomenon is in turn seen as a legacy of certain key assumptions of classical sociological thinking. The social sciences are (or, perhaps, were) one of the most distinctive products of the modernist turn in the humanities. This prompted founding scholars like Durkheim [4] to move programmatically away from the kind of psychologizing sociology that was dominant in the XVIII and early XIX century.

Following to an extent in the steps of Comte, Durkheim conceived society as an object of investigation capable of being understood 'rationally' and 'scientifically'. Historical trends in 'society' too were conceived as moving along a process of increasing rationalization. Having abandoned the irrational, superstitious and prejudiced lead of 'tradition', social institutions and mores were increasingly less indebted to past constraints and governed by formal rationality The inherent quality of society as moving between 'stages' where 'rationality' plays an ever-increasing role became the template of modern sociology. Durkheim's own distinction between 'mechanic' and 'organic' solidarity, Ferdinand Tönnies [5] and others' distinction between 'society' and 'community' – Gesellschaft and Gemeinschaft – Max Weber's [6] views on rationalization as the distinctive feature of 'modern' and 'Western' social formations, still act as a powerful influence on more recent thinkers. Claude Lévi-Strauss [7], with his distinction between 'cold' and 'hot' societies and Norbert Elias' views on the 'civilizing process' (Elias [8]), in fact, follow basically in the

'Tobia', (buildings for storing hay), Val di Fassa, 1930s.
Photograph courtesy of Istitut Cultural Ladin.

same intellectual furrow. To ward off misunderstandings, we must also consider that even conservative thinkers such as José Ortega y Gasset [9] and Arnold Gehlen [10] and all the more Martin Heidegger [11] did subscribe for their part to the notion of a 'rational' and 'scientific' modern age taking over from a 'traditional' past where social life was ruled by cultural norms and values. Only they did not like it.

In the terms of our Conference, in short, there would seem to be in the legacy of the modern social sciences – whether of a progressive or of a conservative kind – an enduring... (I am tempted to say: 'tradition'!) whereby there would be on the one hand social formations dominated by 'tradition' and – on the other hand and quite well ahead in the stream of historical development, for the good or the bad – those societies which underwent, in the words of a contemporary Dutch scholar, the process of 'rational disenchantment' (Spierenburg [12]) on the way to modernity. In this context, Shils' work – being as it is wholly sociologically and not historically oriented – has at least the merit of asking the question of the import of tradition in the fabric of the social body – including, for a change, our own. In 1981 it inaugurated a spate of works which placed the notion of tradition at the centre of both historical and sociological consideration.

3. Global cultural traditions and identity – two examples

The second half of the Seventies witnessed the rediscovery of 'tradition' as the cornerstone for both the construction and the implementation of cultural and social identities. These became suddenly perceived as threatened by modernity for the first time brought under scrutiny and found to be wanting on several accounts. The almost sudden discovery of the evils of globalization did the rest. This did not take place only in the by then hyperdeveloped, so-called 'West', soon to tack round the postmodernist buoy. What was – in my view – one of the first truly symptomatic signs of cultural globalization, entailed that 'cultural traditions' and 'identity' became closely articulated together on a global scale. In particular, the phenomenon known as 'glocalism' pitched a renewed interest in locality, identity and tradition alongside – if not altogether against – the agents of cultural (and other) forms of homogenization. Within the constraints of this paper, I can only offer two examples from my own research, one from Europe and one from Africa.

The Ladins of the Dolomites are one of the many European ethnic minorities to find in the process of European integration an unprecedented opportunity to reassess and vindicate their specific and distinct identity. Wedged in between Italy and Austria, they were overlooked – to the point of becoming historically almost invisible – in the process of formation and historical implementation of what Benedict Anderson terms 'the imagined communities' of the Austrian and the Italian nation-states (Alcock [13]). By the 1970s, the development of one of the strongest service industries in Europe, namely in the form of winter skiing and summer holidaying, had made the Dolomites one of the highest pro-capita income areas of Europe. It was in this context that Ladin militants saw in the increasing economic success the danger of cultural and identity loss (Poppi [14]).

The 1970s saw the growth of an increasingly successful Ladin militancy. The deliberate rediscovery, revival and – occasionally – invention of traditional folk practices sustained the vindication of a distinct identity vis-à-vis Italian- and German-speaking State apparatuses. This operation was conducted most successfully within those cultural domains – such as Carnival, local cuisine, popular religion and so on – where the mandatory presence of an audience – both locals and tourists – boosted the meaning of 'traditional performances' as viable markers of ethnic identity. As I have argued elsewhere, extinct or nearly-extinct cultural practices were resurrected, partly at least, precisely because, having being declared obsolete and redundant by the process of modernization, could function as the evidence of the non-assimilable, irreducible 'otherness' of Ladin cultural identity. The advantage of such practices, in other words, consisted precisely in that they had been 'extinct' for a while and were, therefore, 'inassimilable and non-functional' to current trends (Poppi [15]).

'Tobia', Canazei, Val di Fassa, contemporary photo. Photograph courtesy of Istitut Cultural Ladin.

This process of cultural revival was then a global phenomenon. In the European context alone, it prompted the revision of time-honoured modernist predictions of cultural assimilation to 'the American model'. In drawing appropriate theoretical conclusions from overwhelming ethnographic evidence, anthropologists such as Jeremy Boissevain saw in the ethnic and cultural revival of the Seventies and Eighties the by-product itself of impending globalization. In short: 'identity' was becoming all the more crucial, and its markers of distinction all the more significant, the more the pressure to conform to dominant influences – at all levels of the social fabric – was increasing (Boissevain [16] and [17]; Poppi [18]).

4. The global cultural supermarket
Mutatis mutandis this was also – at least partly – the scenario I was confronted with when I started my research on the Sigma secret society

and cult of masks in a rather peripheral region of Northwestern Ghana in 1985. Here too, a complex interplay between the modernizing undertows of development, local ethnic conflicts and cultural change had triggered by then forms of cultural revival which gave the lie to the prophets of 'assimilationist doom' – if you pass the expression. To cut a long and complex ethnography short, when I underwent the final initiation cycle in the senior ranks of the Sigma secret society in 1995, I estimated that about three hundred people chose to brave nine days in the bush exposed to the scorching sun and spend eight sleepless nights naked in cold temperatures to learn the secret language of the Bush Spirits.

The personnel of the Roman Catholic missions were in some disarray, and their more radical counterparts at the World Evangelical Church station were altogether talking of Devil-lead conspiracies. As a friend put it, the cult that was only a few years before a dim – and dimming – 'survival' of Darkest Africa, lost in a corner of the country not yet reached by school and bore-holes, seemed suddenly to have acquired more customers than a video shop in Lagos.

By and large, such engagements of what were until very recently perceived as marginalized, vanishing and irrelevant cultural practices of a 'traditional' kind, are proving that the negotiation of 'modernity' and 'tradition' is by no means a contest with a foregone conclusion. In particular, evidence is there that what used to be localized, 'ethnically specific' practices, are now putting in a bid to become actors on the world stage, as is for instance the case with the Yoruba religion being systematized to achieve the form of an exportable 'world religion' (e.g. Karade [19]). That this happens – amongst other factors – precisely because such practices enjoy, on the global 'cultural supermarket', credit coming from being 'local' and 'authentic', goes some way in exposing the tangle between the local and the global in the contemporary creation of transcultural values.

We are therefore witnessing the paradox whereby given cultural practices and phenomena which had hitherto been considered by social scientists as the hallmark of dismissal from the process of modernization, are coming back with a vengeance. The hybris of the late phases in the development of world cultural practices – the fact, that is, whereby localized cultural traits are selected, disembedded and re-packaged for larger bodies of consumers – turns into the hybris of the periphery invading the centre and thus inducing the latter to explode into myriad, constantly shifting and self-centred networks.

If this framework is anywhere near being ethnographically accurate, then the juxtaposition of 'tradition' and 'modernity' as differing, contrasting and alternative lifeworlds set head-to-tail in the historical continuum is no longer tenable. In particular, and as this very Conference in itself demonstrates, the reflection on 'tradition' is today an integral part of the rethinking of contemporaneity. As a corollary, like all revisitations, this entails the emergence of a field of what we might call 'cultural pertinence' within which the notion of what exactly tradition is becomes a contested, negotiated and controversial issue. This is the result of changes in the lifeworld, mostly pertinent to the dominant middle classes of the so-called 'West' but slowly making their way elsewhere, whereby the 'collective habitualizations' of old are '…breaking down in a cloud of possibilities to be thought about and negotiated' (Beck and Beck-Gernsheim [20]). The disintegration of habitus into a myriad offers forces self-conscious selectivity, choice and therefore disagreement and conflict – not to mention stress and – often – altogether cultural anomie – whenever such choices come to impinge on matters pertaining to 'the social' (Heelas, Lash and Morris [21]).

5. The ebb and flow of tradition

Thus, presenting tradition as the subject of both reflexive enquiry and practice entails that it immediately becomes a controversial, contested matter. What is 'traditional' for X is grossly out of place and time for Y. What has long entered the canon of the obvious is – for another actor of the social process – unacceptably out of the cultural order. Take for instance the notion of 'the vernacular' in architecture. On the one hand we all know what we mean and we all can name it when we see it. Yet, if we were to try to define a vernacular canon, I am

'Tobià', contemporary photo, Canazei, Val di Fassa. Photograph courtesy of Istitut Cultural Ladin.

certain that we would start arguing as to what constitutes exactly the vernacular tradition in any country. As a ferociously 'traditional' friend of mine from Canton Ticino, in Switzerland, said of Mario Botta's architecture: 'I could not care less if Botta claims to draw inspiration from vernacular architecture: I will not allow him an inch near my old wooden goatshack'.

'Tradition' has just that cognitively slippery, elusive character that enables it to slip through our fingers the moment we try to catch it and pin it down. In this respect, it is more a process than 'a fact', 'an object'. There is no way by which – say – Norman Foster's architecture can be said to be 'traditionally English' – and yet, yet it can be argued that there is something quintessentially 'English' in it. What this is precisely, is difficult – actually: impossible – to tell: either you 'see' it or it is left unsaid. It is not the question here of making a substance of what is, after all, an attribute – that is not the point. The point is that 'tradition' as process entails a kind of fluidity – a state of constant flux of the 'cultural stuff' which is its lifeblood, whereby 'defining' entails 'stopping' and therefore killing it. It comes as no surprise that

'Tobià', contemporary photo, Canazei, Val di Fassa. Photograph courtesy of Istitut Cultural Ladin.

if, having defined and agreed on a 'canon' for tradition, we make an object after that definition, we can only come up with a replica, a copy – ultimately a fake. Thus tradition is never 'done', but always in the making – and strongest where the flow of the tide is allowed to run its cultural course, so to speak.

It was in the assembling stages of the scenario of turning epochal cultural tides outlined above that two bodies of academic work began to grow, both related to a newly acquired taste for 'cultural difference'. On the one hand 'the Other', 'Otherness', 'Othering' and what-not-else became mandatory *topoi* in emerging fields such as cultural and postcolonial studies – and, belatedly as usual, in anthropology and the social sciences too.

6. The invention of traditions

The other body of research, which was to be developed – frankly occasionally ad nauseam – in the next twenty years or so (and it is not over yet!), stemmed from the notion of 'the invention of tradition'. The volume of essays edited by Eric Hobsbawm [22] and Terry Ranger [23], [24] with the title 'The Invention of Tradition' published by Cambridge University Press in 1983 was, arguably, the single most influential work in the social sciences of the latter part of the last millennium. I think it is safe to say that it was prompted phenomenologically by the sudden discovery that 'tradition' – whatever that was – was not only not dead, but alive and kicking hard.

On the other hand, the intellectual noblesse obliged to historicize the concept had to pay duty to the then dominant deconstructivist mood (soon in its turn to become a rather stale tradition in terms of intellectual endeavour). What the deconstruction of the notion of 'tradition' entails is – I think – so well known that it hardly need be summarised. In short: against the assumption that 'traditions' are the long-shadow of the past projected onto the present – un-assimilable, creepy, compulsory and compulsive – 'traditions' should be thought of as constructs best understood in terms of the agendas, desiderata and compulsions of the present. In turning the concept of tradition on its historical head, Hobsbawm [22], Ranger [23], [24] and their associates argued that 'traditions' are 'invented' – from the Latin 'invenire', 'to find' – in two senses.

On the one hand they are 'found' ready made in the lofts of historical memory at times when – so to speak – the lower floors of the house are flooded and cultural militancy needs to find higher and drier grounds.

In a second sense – and more radically – 'traditions' are 'invented' – that is imaginatively forged and fashioned anew – when what I have called elsewhere 'markers of cultural distinctiveness' must be put in place to mark a boundary which suddenly appears, for historical reasons, unmanned and vulnerable (Poppi, [15], [18] and [25]).

At the time when 'deconstruction' was the mandatory war cry of any self-respecting scholar, this reduction to the contemporary of what, for want of a better expression, I would like to term the 'remainders of unsettled historical accounts', became the rage of the day and made a number of illustrious victims. Suddenly, everything was 'invented'. In both senses expounded above – and often in a way that confused the original, rigorous specifications – what were hitherto substantial, objective or simply historically consolidated features in our understanding of social formations, became subjective 'inventions', functional to contemporary agendas.

Thus, Indian castes were claimed to be an 'invention' of British colonial administration bent on finding a way to 'classify' colonial subjects (see Quigley [26] for a critique of such a position). In a similar vein, Italy was the 'invention' of a maverick Piedmontese Count – the reference being here to Camillo Benso Count of Cavour, Italy's Prime Minister at the time – trying to keep a gang of disaffected youths busy by sending them on hopeless expeditions to Sicily. Likewise, the 'invention of tribes' was expedient to the *divide et impera* strategy of European imperialism. I even remember reading worried rallying cries quickly to invent ' traditions of Englishness' as the English were loosing out to the Scots, the Welsh, the Manxonians and who else in the race to allocate the shards of a shattered British identity.

Flour mill, XVIII century, presently a section of the Ladin Museum, Pera di Fassa, Val di Fassa. Photograph courtesy of Istitut Cultural Ladin.

Map showing the distribution of the Ladins in the Alps.

7. De-historicizing history

Of the many, complex issues raised by this kind of approach to the problem of cultural continuity, I wish here to discuss only a general – and paradoxical – theoretical consequence. What began as a dutiful, powerful and legitimate attempt both to give substance to- and to historicize a concept until then deployed in a loose, unguarded and intellectually weak sense, ended up by de-historicizing history itself.

This is to say that, by reducing the import of the legacy of the past to a matter of contemporary strategies, the past was made to be altogether a function of the present. What counts possibly as the leading epistemological paradigm in the constitution of modern historiography, as expressed in Wilhelm Dilthey's [27] methodology, asserted that meaningful interpretations of historic events are possible through an 'emphatic understanding' whose plausibility rests upon the assumption of the common humanity of both the protagonists of the *res gestae* and the interpreters of their actions. The possibility of an intersubjectively valid 'historiographic truth', therefore, rested upon what was – in the last instance – a psychological argument. Rightly or wrongly that this might be, it implied that the present – including the intellectual tools forged in understanding the past – was the result of past actions, and as such it had to be considered by a self-comprehending methodology.

The methodological thrust of postmodernist historiography turns all this on its head. In predicating that the past is basically a construction of present agendas and desiderata, it favours theoretical relativism and methodological subjectivism. Having made of the past a foreign country, then the process of *verstehen* is encapsulated within the constraints of the present – no assumption of an underlying psychological, cultural or other form of underlying unity being there to keep the flow – as it were – between 'the thens' and 'the nows' of the historiographic enterprise. Unlike Dilthey and his followers' attempt to subsume the *verstehen* of the knowing subject as a constitutive – if problematic – variable in historiography itself, postmodernist historiography ends up by de-historicizing the problem of the positioning of the knowing subject – and the possibility of locating it in an intersubjectively valid point of view which would salvage the possibility of a 'truthful' account of history. Following in the furrow of the subjectivist thrust of late modern philosophy (Habermas [28]), and in spite of its protestations, contemporary theory sees the subject's 'positioning' in history as an insurmountable ontological problem and not – as it was in 'classic' historiography – a problem of gnoseology subsumable – and possibly solvable – in the process of *verstehen*. In this way, postmodernism sets the issue of methodological and theoretical solipsism beyond the reach of critical scrutiny: every reading of history is, by definition, located, but such locatedness is transcendental and beyond the reach of critical subsumption for it is constitutive of the subject itself.

It is easy to see how, in this way, what began as an attempt critically to throw light on the ideological and expedient use of the then past, ends up by prejudicially (and self-deceptively!) emptying the *res gestae* of the capacity – for the better or worse – to inject their unsettling, autonomous, problematic and often ominous legacy into the present.

This is achieved by declaring them an entirely subjective construction where the line between *res gestae* and *res imaginariae* is blurred and finally snaps.

It is – I think – the awareness of such unintended consequences and implications of intended actions that prompted Terence Ranger [23] to write a famous, courageous essay at the peak of the deconstructivist tide. In 'The Invention of Tradition Revisited: The Case of Colonial Africa' of 1993, he provided a series of *caveat emptors* aimed at the all-too enthusiastic subscribers of the new trends. In a nutshell, what Ranger argued here against the excesses of subjectivists and reductionist understandings of long-term cultural continuities, is that they owe their functionality to the power struggle and the political agendas of the present in the first place to the fact that they have a real, 'objective' and irreducible purchase over the subjects jostling about the power – to use Pierre Bourdieu's expression – 'to make people see and believe' (Bourdieu [29]).

Thus, for instance, 'tribal identity' in Southern Africa was not simply an instrument of control available to colonial settlers and their administration. As a primary marker of identity, it also functioned – as it still does – as a rallying point – symbolic and other – for collective actions of resistance.

Language – in the case of European ethnic minorities – is not simply the 'found', expedient 'invention' of ethnic militants bent on enforcing their distinctiveness. As a primary means of socialization, language can be deployed as a marker of distinctiveness precisely because it is not invented, but formed through time and given to each generation – if admittedly wholly historically (but what isn't 'historically given' anyway?) – as a building block of identity which transcends – in a Kantian, non-ontological sense – the building process itself.

8. Structured tradition

In this sense, 'tradition' is all the more consequential an effect of social and cultural continuity, liable moreover to be pressed into service in times of social change, when the struggle to enforce new balances in the social fabric is in need of meaningful constructs – whether of a symbolical or of an institutional kind – to signal a crisis in the balance of power.

This revised, more balanced and nuanced understanding of the 'invention of tradition' is paralleled, in the growing and promising field of cognitive anthropology, by a renewed interest in understanding 'tradition' as a structural process whereby cultural constructs are imbued with legitimacy and communicated between generations. It is these developments that will be briefly illustrated, as they will open the way to Conclusions.

Water-powered saw mill, XIX century, presently a section of the Ladin Museum, Penia, Val di Fassa. Photograph courtesy of Istitut Cultural Ladin.

9. Justifying tradition

Anthropologists are often confronted with the apparent incapacity of their 'informants' to provide the reasons for this or that cultural practice. It has become almost an academic cliché to say that no justification can be provided for core cultural practices other than: 'This is our custom. We do this because our forefathers did so, our mothers did so and our children will continue to do so too'. If that kind of statement lays to rest the semiological deciphering frenzy of the anthropologist – or at least it so does, in my experience, from the Dolomites to Northern Ghana – when taken seriously it can highlight the crucial cognitive function of seemingly unfathomable concepts such as 'tradition'. In a study titled 'Tradition as Truth and Communication', anthropologist Pascal Boyer [30] has written perhaps the first attempt to give an account of what anthropologists have been told countless times and only mistook for the incapacity to articulate 'the meaning' of cultural behaviour.

Against this, it can be argued that, very often, it is the most crucial and salient 'symbolic utterances' of a given social formation that are entrenched by the actors of the social process within the cultural recesses – if you pass the expression – of the notion of 'tradition'. Moreover, it is especially the most counter-intuitive of such utterances which are selected for such treatment.

'Tobià', Antermont, Val di Fassa, 1950s.
Photograph courtesy of Istitut Cultural Ladin.

In other words, the more a given cultural trait is questionable at the level of common sense, and the more – on the contrary – it is crucial for the functioning of the social fabric, the more it is likely to be treated as 'justified by tradition'. For instance, the Vagla people with whom I work in Northern Ghana do not kill fruit bats (otherwise an excellent and abundant source of proteins) because they maintain that bats host the souls of their ancestors. They know, however, that the neighbouring Lobi do eat bats, and this is a powerful enforcer of the opinion that the Lobi are savages. In their turn, the Lobi say that the Vagla are primitive because they believe that bats are their ancestors and ignore that it is hippopotamuses instead who harbour our forefathers.

In this sense, therefore, counterintuitive, 'unbelievable beliefs' act as powerful markers of identity – and the more 'irrational' the more salient they will be. But, if their function towards the outside is to mark a boundary, internally the function of such 'cultural utterances' is to support authority by providing a – literally unquestionable – process of truth-validation.

In social formations where oral tradition is the only way explicitly to communicate cultural values between generations, the only 'terminal of tradition' one is confronted with – and the only one can eventually question – is the current 'elder in charge', the 'last in line' of the tradition in question – as it were.

10. Origins of tradition

As in a fibre optic, one can only and always have an idea of the source of given information at its terminal end – as it were. Unlike the case with written sources, one cannot go back to 'the original text' and query the conformity of its contemporary rendering from that vantage point. There are of course disputes about what constitutes 'tradition' amongst elders and other such 'authorities', but these are conducted from the same standpoint of 'optic fibre'-like terminals. In this sense, therefore, what ultimately and forcibly has to decide what version will prevail is the current balance of power between competing 'terminals' of tradition. The rest is forgotten.

Contesting tradition does not per se change the nature of the cognitive process of validation of a given utterance. In such circumstances, there are no textual and philological 'inaccuracies', but only 'moral lies'. In this respect, it is significant that philosophers like Plato did not trust committing a text to writing: writings could be altered and forged, but oral tradition would preserve the integrity of the original rendering because – once the pedigree of the utterer was accepted – it would be literally unquestionable.

If this is the case, we can argue that the notion of 'tradition' works as the validatory mechanism of certain, selected cultural utterances. Furthermore, it also provides the cognitive mechanism by which such utterances are passed on from generation to generation. While supplying authority with a measure of legitimacy, at the same time they appear to preserve the 'freshness' and the 'authenticity' of their original source. As a Vagla friend of mine put it: 'I do not know who said that the Sigma masks are bush spirits, nor do I know where, when or why. What I know is that someone, somewhere, sometime said so. This has been true for a long time and it is not a lie today'.

In the words of my Vagla friend, 'tradition' is thus a means of 'telescoping truth' back to its original, authoritative source by transcending time as the process itself which makes tradition. A way, if you prefer, both to negotiate the meaning of the past and accommodate its impact upon the present.

11. Conclusion

By way of conclusion, I have argued in this paper that 'tradition' began to be taken seriously when modernist dominant paradigms in the social sciences reached the critical turn of the Seventies. It was then, under the pressure of globalizing processes, that new views and new practices began to emerge, in the field, concerning the ways by which the past becomes inextricably entangled with the present. Early rediscoveries of 'tradition' deconstructed the wilful and deliberate reappropriation of the past as dictated by wholly contemporary agendas.

The understanding of the past in terms of 'the invention of tradition', I have argued, was meant to historicize tradition but ended up – paradoxically – by flattening the historical perspective and folding it over, as it were, onto the contemporary.

In the final part of this paper, I have instead argued that a more balanced perspective on 'tradition' can be achieved if we see in it a specific cognitive mechanism. Through its operations authority is upheld by validating the truth-content of critical cultural utterances, while a mechanism is provided for communicating both them and their sources along the generational continuum.

In 1992 I wrote: 'In general, the "reasons" of history are "invented" by historical subjects, but they appoint their own cast of characters. Each generation finds the conditions upon which to operate as a conscious subject already set by its predecessors, in a form which appears to its actor as objectively given: each generation's agenda is written on the former's (Poppi 1992 [15]).

Ten years on, I would like to think that critically understanding the legacy of the past as both what our present condition enables us to perceive, but also as the grinder of the mirror through which we look back, constitutes the proper way to approach tradition.

References

[1] Shils, E. 1981, *Tradition*, London, Faber.

[2] Gross, D. 1991, *The past in Ruins: Tradition and the Critique of Modernity*, Amherst, University of Massachusetts Press.

[3] Pelikan, J. 1984, *The Vindication of Tradition*, New Haven, Yale University Press.

[4] Durkheim, E. 1895, *Les Règles de la methode sociologique*, Paris, Germer Baillière.

[5] Tönnies, F. 1979, *Gemeinschaft und Gesellschaft: Grundbegriffe der reinen Soziologie*, Darmstadt, Wissenschaftliche Buchgesellschaft.

[6] Weber, M. 2001, *The Protestant Ethic and the Spirit of Capitalism*, Chicago, Fitzroy Dearborn.

[7] Lévi-Strauss, C. 1973, *Anthropologie Structurale*, 2 vols, Paris, Plon.

[8] Elias, N. 1982, *The Civilizing Process*, 2 vols, New York, Pantheon Books.

[9] Ortega y Gasset, J. 1941, *Toward a Philosophy of History*, New York, W.W. Orton & Co.

[10] Gehlen, A. 1980, *Man in the Age of Technology*, New York, Columbia University Press.

[11] Heidegger, M. 1977, *The Question Concerning Technology and Other Essays*, London, Harper and Low.

[12] Spierenburg, P. 1991, *The Broken Spell: a Cultural and Anthropological History of Preindustrial Europe*, New Brunswick, Macmillan.

[13] Alcock, A.E. 1970, *The History of the South Tyrol Question*, London, Joseph.

[14] Poppi, C. 2001, *The Ladins: People of the Pale Mountains*, Dublin, The European Bureau for lesser used languages.

[15] Poppi, C. 1992, 'Building Difference: the Political Economy of Tradition in the Ladin Carnival of the Val di Fassa', In J. Boissevain (ed.), *Revitalizing European Rituals*, London, Routledge.

[16] Boissevain, J. (ed.) 1992, *Revitalizing European Rituals*, London, Routledge.

[17] Boissevain, J. (ed.) 1996, *Coping with Tourists: European Responses to Mass Tourism*, Oxford, Berghan Books.

[18] Poppi, C. 1997, 'Wider Horizons with Larger Details: Subjectivity, Ethnicity and Globalization', in A. Scott (ed.), *The Limits of Globalization*, London, Routledge.

[19] Karade, I. 1991, *The Handbook of Yoruba Religious Concepts*, East Orange, N.J., Weiser Books.

[20] Beck, U. and Beck-Gernsheim, 1996, 'Individualization and Precarious Freedoms', in P. Heelas, S. Lash and P. Morris (eds), *Detraditionalization: critical reflections on authenticity and identity*, Oxford, Blackwell.

[21] Heelas, P., Lash, S. and Morris, P. (eds) 1996, *Detraditionalization: Critical Reflections on Authority and Identity*, Oxford, Blackwell.

[22] Hobsbawm, E. and Ranger, T. (eds) 1983, *The Invention of Tradition*, Cambridge, Cambridge University Press.

[23] Ranger, T. 1993, 'The Invention of Tradition Revisited: The Case of Colonial Africa', in T. Ranger and O. Vaughan (eds), *Legitimacy and the State in Twentieth-Century Africa*, London, Macmillan Press.

[24] Ranger, T. and Vaughan, O. 1993, *Legitimacy and the State in Twentieth-Century Africa*, London, Macmillan Press.

[25] Poppi, C. 1991, 'The Contention of Tradition: Legitimacy, Culture and Ethnicity in Southern Tyrol', in AA.VV. *Per Padre Frumenzio Ghetta…*, Trento/Vich, Institut Cultural Ladin.

[26] Quigley, D. 1997. 'Deconstructing Colonial Fiction? Some Conjuring Tricks in the Recent Sociology of India', in A. James *et al.* (eds), *After Writing Culture*, London, Routledge.

[27] Dilthey, 1996, *Hermeneutics and the Study of History*, Princeton, Princeton University Press.

[28] Habermas, J. 1987, *The Philosophical Discourse of Modernity*, Oxford, Blackwell.

[29] Bourdieu, P. 1982, *Ce Que Parler Veut Dire: l'Économie des Échanges Linguistiques*, Paris, Fayard.

[30] Boyer, P. 1990, *Tradition as Truth and Communication: a Cognitive Description of Traditional Discourse*, Cambridge, Cambridge University Press.

Religion and Tradition: Patterns of Migration, Conversion and Enculturation within Globalisation and Cultural Change

Clive Erricker

> *He who controls the present controls the past and*
> *he who controls the past controls the future.*
> (Orwell, 1984)

CLIVE ERRICKER

Clive Erricker is County Inspector for Religious Education in Hampshire, UK. Previously he was Reader in Religious Education and Head of the Study of Religions in University College Chichester. He is joint editor of the International Journal of Children's Spirituality, Co-director of the Children and Worldviews Project and author and editor of a number of books on contemporary spirituality, religion in the modern world and religious and spiritual education.

1. Introduction: what is tradition and what is tradition for?

The above quotation, from Orwell's *Animal Farm,* can be readily applied to the way, historically, religious traditions have exercised influence and power, in a similar manner to other ideologies. But, the world in the twenty-first century is likely to be a time of challenge to religion and by religion. Tradition is central to the character of institutionalised religious life by virtue of being the instrument by which religion achieves stability and, as a result, the ability to meet new challenges as societies develop new forms.

Religious traditions, the two terms are often married in this phrase, are those institutions that seek to preserve the continuing relevance of religion to modern life. But, the place of religion in modern western society is in decline, at least in so far as the influence traditional religion has on the lifestyles of citizens and the politics and values of nation states. England represents a particularly interesting case in this respect with its long standing relationship between state and established church. Tradition conserves and renews; it provides continuity within the process of change. It constructs 'orthodoxies' to preserve 'truths' within this context.

Nevertheless, although religious traditions are most usually identified from without as being rigid and solid: immovable rather than flexible objects, their survival and their influence demand flexibility.

We might compare them more to candle flames than to fortresses in so far as, preserving the contour of their form, they shift continually in response to the elemental conditions that prevail on them and within them. Religious traditions have to take account of the new, even if there is a tendency to resist it.

Paradoxically, this can even mean they become a part of the new, having an increasing influence in the modern world by virtue of the appeal generated by reconfiguration, or just 're-branding'; as for example with the Alpha movement in the Christian Church. Conversion to high-profile forms of both Christianity and Islam provide other recent examples. Crucial to the maintenance of tradition in religion is the relationship that exists between the religion and its 'host' culture; its economic base, and its appeal to successive generations. To illustrate these points, specific case studies are presented that relate to Buddhism and Islam. To highlight the issues involved these studies throw into relief the problems and possibilities arising from migration and conversion.

2. Migrant religion and conversion in Buddhism

The growth of the Buddhist presence in the West in the latter half of the twentieth century has been cumulative and diverse, such that it is possible to find or indeed commit yourself to, a representative range of any form of Buddhism found across the globe: Tibetan, Zen, Pure Land, Nichiren, Theravadin, for example. Beyond this there are also the seeds of seeking to establish forms of western Buddhism, as traditional forms adapt to new cultural settings or, as in the case of the Western Buddhist Order, create a distinct form that is free of alien cultural characteristics from its inception. There are also Buddhist groups that cross traditional Buddhist divides and welcome the pluralism of the western situation as a positive enriching development. This situation has developed into a fascinating picture of religious, social and cultural change, which is still in its infancy. Within this the question of contemporary spiritual values is a key factor.

2. 1 The Buddhist Forest Retreat Order

The Forest Retreat Order represents one of the most traditional forms of Buddhist transplantation and for that reason, paradoxically perhaps in its new setting, one of the most radical alternatives to conventional western lifestyles and values. How does a Thai *Sangha* (Buddhist monastic community) based on the strict observance of the *Vinaya* (code of conduct) and accustomed to remote rural territory flourish in the west?

Documentation of the growth of Ajahn Chah's Thai Forest Retreat Order in the West is now readily available in scholarly works. Its beginnings resided in his own disaffection with the state of Buddhism in Thailand after receiving monastic ordination at the age of twenty-one in 1939. The study of Buddhist doctrine and *Pali* texts within his training brought him no closer to realising the Buddha's emphasis on the teachings having one aim: the cessation of suffering. The laxness of the practice by *bhikkhus* (Buddhist monks) and lay people alike was equally uninspiring. Such disenchantment, which actually threads throughout the movement as an inspiration and is echoed later, led to Ajahn Chah's meeting with the meditation master Ajahn Mun, his subsequent *dhutanga* (travels as a mendicant) of seven years in the forests and jungles of Thailand and his conviction as to the importance of the monastic rule and the practice of mindfulness as 'seeing that everything arises in one's own heart'. The forcefulness of this insight and its abiding presence in the movement is testified to in a piece of recent monkish graffiti on the workshop door of Amaravati, their largest monastery and centre in the United Kingdom. It reads: 'mindfulness leads to the deathless, heedlessness leads to death', expressed with the same stark force and directness as Ajahn Chah used in his darsanas (teachings). This is a paraphrase of verse 21 of the *Dhammapada* [2] that reads as follows:

> Mindfulness is the path to the deathless;
> Heedlessness is the path to death.
> The mindful do not die;
> But the heedless are as if dead already.

Also, this can be found as a prologemia to Ajahn Sumedho's teachings in *Mindfulness: The Path to the Deathless* [3] and thus alerts us to the significance of the maintenance of tradition in the teachings and practices in the present Order, which gives to it direction and sustenance in its present situation, despite or perhaps because of increasing social and cultural diversity.

In an invaluable piece of social documentary the BBC filmed 'When the Buddha Comes to Sussex' [4], a chronicle of these beginnings. Apart from showing the original restorative work of the monks and acting as an introduction to traditional Buddhist practice, it signals the initial impact of an alien spiritual presence within the historic rural preserve of genteel middle class English conservatism. In a parody of difference each plays their part with commitment and concern.

The sorts of anxieties expressed and misunderstandings that ensued exemplify many of the difficulties involved in the transmutation of traditional monocultural localities into acceptance of the pluralism of the larger world. In this case the peculiarity of encounter resided in

Evelyn Chiao: Inside of the Great Ummayad Mosque, Aleppo, Syria 2006. Reproduced by permission of the artist.

the coming together of two traditional ways of life that were new to each other by virtue of the geographical and cultural distance that had always separated them. In other words it was the shock of encountering another form of tradition that created the shock of the new, at least insofar as rural Sussex was concerned. It was the importance of the *Vinaya* to the Forest Order that created the sense of disorientation and concern, as it manifested itself in the distinctive presence and activity of the saffron robed community. Comments made by local residents at a meeting organised by the local vicar and elsewhere 'on location' illustrate the difficulties involved in the acceptance of 'otherness' and the ways in which it is understood. The following comments are illustrative of this:

> This little hamlet…has been steeped in the Christian religion for hundreds of years…even the ground…is steeped in Christianity…this is an intrusion, an invasion…they are all searching for something. We've got what we want. We've got a God, always had a God.

> I think it's all right provided they keep to themselves. I don't know what they are doing now, searching for food or something…I disapprove of that frightfully.

> I think this is the most remarkable event that this hall has ever seen and I'm quite prepared to wake up tomorrow and find it was all a dream. What we want to know is how large is the community and how many hangers on are there.

> The only reason people are asking you questions is because you're different…dressed in your funny gear. Good luck to you if you can make a go of it and get something for nothing. I mean it.

This raises the issue of why there was no previous adaptation decided upon by the Order before locating themselves in such an environment. Ajahn Sumedho's comments on this are instructive both at a practical and spiritual level. They are indicative of the significance of tradition.

We are a tradition that believes itself to be from the original…and we are limiting our lives to the boundaries of the Vinaya…to get us to reflect on our impulsivity, assumptions, cultural habits…alms mendicancy is an act of faith. We seek to live within the limitations it confers and reflect daily…and be grateful for what we are given: food, clothing, shelter, medicine being made available to you. Our lives have to depend on the good heartedness of the lay community. If the lay community isn't good hearted, then we wouldn't be able to exist…this allows us to maintain meditation: the spiritual exercises that we have.

(Interview with the author, 15 December 1999, Amaravati).

The Forest Retreat Order represents a tale of tradition renewed or reconstructed, having fallen into decline. Adaptation is minimal upon migration. Its characteristics have been referred to as 'Protestant Buddhism' because the impetus for renewal in Thailand was originally generated by a western convert and similar to the inception of the Christian Protestant Churches in Europe, the aim was to restore the 'original' faith that had been corrupted and diminished.

The Order's appeal is to a western disaffection with a secularised society that lacks spiritual incentive and motivation. The spiritual example of monks and nuns living the monastic life with a high degree of discipline based on renunciation is the main attraction.

This example we might refer to as 'regenerated tradition' deliberately setting out not to integrate itself with the norms of its 'host' culture.

2.2 The Japanese Buddhist church of America

This movement provides an interesting comparison with the above. In Tetsuden Kashima's study of Japanese Buddhists in the United States (Kashima [5]), we find a story which can be paralleled by other immigrant groups' histories; for example, those of Vietnamese Buddhists, Bangladeshi and Khojas Shi'a Ithnasheeri Muslims and various Hindu and Sikh communities. The author is of Japanese extraction and the son of a priest, the Reverend Tetsuro Kashima, of the Japanese Buddhist Churches of America. In this study we can trace an example of Buddhist ethnic transference to the West, which is comparatively rarely documented in Buddhism when compared to the studies of transmigration that has occurred with ethnic groups in other religions.

Kashima remarks on how 'The Buddhist Church of America (BCA) represents an alien religion in America – one that has continued for seventy-six years'. It is predominantly Jodo Shinshu of the West and East School varieties and most emigrated from the Hiroshima area (Prefecture), representing a quarter of the total migrants who numbered 84,562. The Buddhist Churches of America represents Jodo Shinshu (Amida Buddhism or Pure Land) with its headquarters in San Francisco. It was inaugurated under this name in 1944 after the traumatic events during the Second World War when almost all the Japanese and Nisei (first generation Americans of Japanese ancestry) were interned. This resulted in a complete dislocation of habits and lifestyles. A continual theme in the history of the institution is its importance as a force for ethnic solidarity, 'The Buddhist Church is a place for the Japanese to meet other Japanese' as one Nisei father stated. In this respect it existed solely for the Japanese and their offspring since 1899. The use of the word church has become increasingly problematic for its members during the latter decades of the 20th Century since it does not reflect the purposes or structures of an inherently Japanese Buddhist religious community. As Kashima points out, Temple or Dojo ('a place where the Way is cultivated') is a more proper description of its place of worship, and sangha is a more exact description of its membership ([5]:187).

The history of Japanese immigrants bears some familiar features. Prejudice and wilfully ignorant racism such as that propagated by the Western Central Labor Union in Seattle in 1900 whose propagation for restrictions on immigration led to such descriptions of Japanese Buddhists as having the 'treacherous, sneaking, insidious, betraying and perfidious nature and characteristics of the Mongolian race' ([5]: 18).

Kashima suggests that the use of the word 'church' was probably an attempt to mitigate against anti-Japanese agitation and is evidence of the Americanisation of second and third generation Japanese.

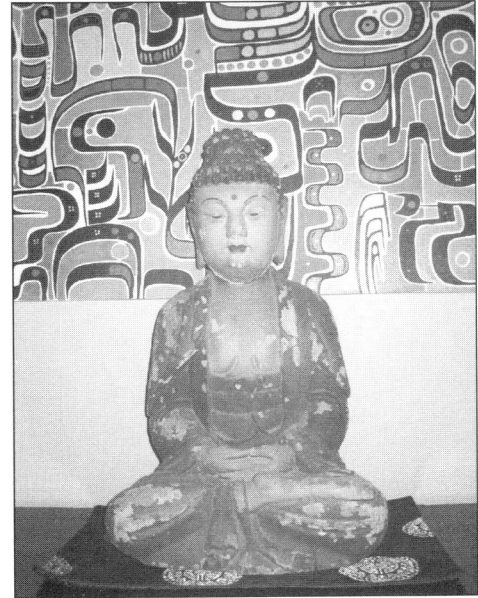

Antique Chinese Buddha with contemporary painting by Amini Kourosh (Xerxes, 2005) in background. Private collection.

The Japanese bombing of Pearl Harbor in December 1941, despite its condemnation by the Buddhist Mission of North America (as it then was) led to internment. Most of those interned were Buddhists. Even before the bombing 'Many Japanese destroyed items that might be regarded as incriminating: some burned sutra books (scriptures), while others concealed their family Buddhist altars.' ([5]: 48)

With generational change from Issei to Nisei to Sansei (3rd generation, but second generation American born) the membership declined in relation to the size of the Japanese American population since the BCA never systematically proselytised and successive generations did not have the same need for its support as members of an ethnic minority. Also, those who still belonged to and supported the organisation did not necessarily practice Buddhism. One Nisei minister commenting on why there was continued Nisei involvement with their church suggested:

> Perhaps it could be guilt or family pressure. What my parents have done for the temple, and therefore...I must carry on. And the other one would say I must do it for my children. These may be some of the reasons why they do it. But not so much from the religious standpoint. ([5]: 188)

A Nisei said, 'I don't know anything about Buddhism, I'll come not to the service but to other things. To carnivals, but not to study class or the *Hondo* [temple hall].' ([5]: 188)

Kashima remarks on the differences among the three generations as highlighted by the Reverend Koshin Ogui:

> As history shows, the Issei had to work to support their families, nothing but work. The Nisei were educated by the Issei to build up their lives the same as the *hakujin* [Caucasian] people. So you see the majority of Nisei people out to buy cars and homes. They don't think about spiritual matters. They are more satisfied with fancy cars and homes. The Sansei are raised in such a background and getting tired of it. Of course, they respect their families. But they're looking for more importance in life – to go forward to fight for human rights, against

racial discrimination and to help the community instead of building up their abundance. ([5]: 197)

If this proves to be the case and the BCA extends its involvement with other non-Japanese Shin-Buddhists, the spiritual heart of the organisation could be re-vitalised.

But Kashima's judgement is equivocal, 'Looking ahead we may conceive of many futures for the BCA, which is really just another way of saying that the future is uncertain.' He also refers to the remarks of the historian H.A.L. Fisher as being highly applicable to this situation:

> One intellectual excitement has...been denied me. Men wiser and more learned than I have discovered in history a plot, a rhythm, a predetermined pattern. These harmonies are concealed from me. I can see only one emergency following another, as wave follows upon wave, only one great fact with respect to which, since it is unique, there can be no generalisation...the play of the contingent and the unforeseen. ([5]: 205)

Kashima suggests that possible futures depend on how a number of present problems are resolved, he cites five: decreasing and changing membership; the ethnic character of membership; economic problems; the proper techniques for teaching Buddhism; interrelated problems with the ministry. All of the problems are ultimately interconnected, as he observes ([5]: 207). He also posits that if the BCA comes to include a wider racial representation, as its leaders envision, then 'Buddhism will indeed become fully Americanised' ([5]: 220).

What is interesting in this study, is the close but shifting connections between ethnicity (Japanese), nationality (American), and religiosity (Buddhist) representing the equation that the community has to balance across three generations. For each generation the balance between these factors is different, in terms of priority. Migration was one of the dominant features of the twentieth century and is likely to be no less dominant in the twenty-first. It determines the issues of particular importance to this Buddhist group; it creates future uncertainty, discrimination, and problems in distinguishing the relationship between religion and culture, a relationship that changes across generations. Is being Buddhist important, as an aspect of identity, in a secularised American environment? Is it better to shed it in the movement towards becoming fully American, or is it the vital commitment to be retained and nurtured, against all others, to preserve identity and values? What does being Buddhist actually mean for this community and how does it relate to larger issues concerning the spiritual and moral condition of a globalised world in the twenty-first century? What does the propagation of the dharma mean for this kind of community when its initial concern for the first, migrant, generation was economic survival and ethnic identity, then, for the next generation, wealth creation and assimilation? The questions that emerge for an immigrant group of this kind differ to those posed for Buddhists in other situations. When Kashima speaks of anticipating Buddhism becoming fully Americanised what sort of Buddhism will this be?

When migration is principally concerned with the preserving of ethnic tradition the result, it seems, is the failure of religious tradition to inspire the same spiritual values and practices in future generations. Comparing the two Buddhist movements suggests that religious tradition becomes rejuvenated when there is a renewal of spiritual vision that attracts new blood through conversion. Thus, tradition itself depends for its survival on the correct balance of dynamic and judicious change and stasis. But it must be wary of corroding factors associated with both the preservation of an 'ethnic' culture and assimilation into a new 'national' culture.

3. A Muslim comparison: the Khoja Shi'a Ithnasheeris

What needs to be preserved and what needs to be changed in relation to custom, belief and ritual? How are shifts in identity accomplished without the loss of religious identity? Let us now consider the issues raised by the Buddhist examples in relation to a Muslim group.

What are we? All our communities are called Khoja Shi'a Ithnasheeri. But first is Khoja. We are Khojas because that is our tribe, Shi'as because that is what our belief is and then Ithnasheeri because we follow the 12 Imams. Until about 23 years ago, every community was naming itself differently and we said let's standardize the whole thing. Today it has worked out at a slight disadvantage, if someone is looking for us as a Muslim community in the telephone directory they will never find us! They would look under M for Muslim and we are never there.

(Jaffer Dharamsi, interview with the author, 28 February 2000, Stanmore, Middlesex, UK.)

This statement would not seem to pressage an auspicious beginning. It suggests the Khoja (ethnic) identity precedes the Muslim (religious) one. However, this community is taking account of its inherent associated problems. Its emphasis is on being Shi'a, the spiritual values of Shi'a Islam and the importance it places on religious freedom. This is a familiar theme in its history of migration.

The primary reason we left India was a religious one, because of our religious practices, not having freedom in this respect. In Zanzibar it was different. There were mosques everywhere, there was a common greeting and that really made all the Khojas feel at home. This was not so on the mainland. We could not blend in with the local tribes in Kenya because they were not Muslim. That was the difference. And since then, it has been a struggle to blend in with the local culture: in the west, in Kenya, in Tanzania because the majority of the population is Christian. The single factor that allowed us that freedom was common religious practice. In situations where we find the practices contradict ours, we become more cautious. For example, you will not find Khojas socialising with natives of this country because the practices are different. The same was true in Mombassa [Kenya] where they drink alcohol and eat pork.

(Shaik Mustafa Jaffer, interview with the author, 28 February 2000, Stanmore, Middlesex, UK.)

David Apthorp: Painting of mosque, 1996–1998. Reproduced by permission of PSTA.

The challenges presented in the West are, arguably, much greater than those presented in East Africa. These challenges relate most specifically to the upbringing of first generation Khoja children. Jaffer Dharamsi explains this by contrasting his own upbringing in Zanzibar with that of Khoja children in the United Kingdom:

> After school they go and play with their friends and they offer them something to eat and drink and they have to say no. You see it all presents problems. For me in Zanzibar I used to go to a friend's house, he would come to my house. Food was not a problem; girl boy separation was not a problem. For our children it is something they have to deal with and we try to teach them how to deal with it.

> *(Jaffer Dharamsi, interview with the author, 28 February 2000, Stanmore, Middlesex, UK.)*

But the problems experienced in the West now seem to bear similarity with those found in traditional Islamic countries, given the influence of globalisation.

> 'My father says I am free to express myself to him. But I can't because our culture dictates that young people do not assert themselves before their elders,' says Hussain. 'Heavy metal is my only outlet. All my pent up energy is released when I listen to it.' (del Nevo [6]: 3)

Hussain, from Lahore in Pakistan, is a 19-year-old urban, middle class boy with a desire to be a journalist. He further remarks, 'In the West a boy of my age can make his own choices...He can talk to girls, drink, listen to any type of music. We don't necessarily want to indulge in these things. But we do want the freedom to choose. And our parents don't understand – they feel threatened.' ([6]: 3)

The significant issue in the difference between his experience and that of his understanding of children in the West is one of being in a culture that you feel you have some ownership of and one where you can create your own separate sub-culture. But Muslim children in the West voice similar concerns to his. For example, this 11 year old Khoja boy:

> Although I agree with my dad, sometimes I feel that we live on two different planets. He has not been to the same school as I have...and he has no idea regarding what my friends get up to or watch on TV or read. My friends – I have so many non-Muslim friends – seem to be having so much fun and I feel at times that I am being forced not to enjoy...At home they (my friends) can do whatever they like...My life seems to be filled so much with trying to be a Muslim than enjoying without worry. So much fuss being a Muslim. (Erricker [7]:216)

It falls to the present adult generation to negotiate this sense of difference and determine the impact of it on tradition. The next generation will have to do likewise. For Khoja Shia's the need to preserve identity in the context of new cultural influences has made the Jamaat (local religious community), as a centre of worship and a place of belonging, a critical force for survival. But the question as to how it competes with wider cultural influences that attract the youth in their search for identity remains an open one. Here we have a situation comparable to that of the Japanese Buddhists in America, but the secular influence has now spread further afield. There is no longer insularity from it based on religious and national identity, per se. Religious tradition has to cope with the pressures of cultural globalisation across the former territorial borders within which nationality and religious identity were more securely related.

One religion that has been familiar with these sorts of problems for some time is Judaism.

In their recent study of Jewish continuity in the USA, *The Next Generation: Jewish Children and Adolescents* (Keysar, Kosmin and Scheckner [8]), and the authors comment that:

> Involvement in Jewish life and the organized community generally requires significant sums of money...Given a parental commitment to Jewish socialization, children in households with a higher per capita income not only are given more options to enrich their life, but also

more opportunity to develop, bond, and connect with their heritage, and become more involved with the Jewish community. ([8]: 32)

However, they also cite Winter's observation that:

The decision of whether or not to affiliate to a synagogue…is not solely a consequence of family income. (It) is apt to be dependent both on family income…and on the degree of Jewish identity or commitment.

(Winter [9]:149; [8]:33)

Relating the analysis of Jewish community to the Khoja Shia's we can identify three important factors in ensuring continuity. A high level of secular education of the youth to equip them for professional employment or self-employment, which will perpetuate future sufficient household per capita income to maintain and develop organized community life; effective religious or faith education to perpetuate commitment to religious identity; and marriage relations. Since unsuccessful marriage results in lower income for one parent families ([8]: 26-32) and thus limits the options available and marriage outside the Khoja, Shi'a or wider Muslim community will weaken commitment and thus the religiosity or sense of Shi'a Muslim identity in the family. However, it is worth noting that synagogue attendance in the Jewish tradition is in decline and there is some foreboding as to the future of the established Jewish religious traditions.

4. The construct of tradition: its future and its purposes

What can be concluded from these brief observations? Is it the case that religious tradition is, in itself, disappearing? Probably not, this was far more of an expectation in the nineteenth century than it is in the twenty-first. Despite changes in cultural identity, in social identity and in national identity, all of which are increasingly complex, religion is a pervasive force. But, in the waxing and waning of its influence some factors appear particularly significant. Change in the cultural and social landscape is inevitable and accommodation of change is

Shafon Miah – Wooden inlay mihrab, 2001–2003.
Reproduced by permission of PSTA.

often seen as a positive response. However, this has not served the nineteenth century reform movements in Judaism very well, or the reform movements in Christianity, both Methodism and the Baptist Church are in decline. One could say that the more resistant dogmatism of Orthodox Judaism, Orthodox and Roman Catholic Christianity have fared better in terms of allegiance over time. Renewal, through revisiting an idea of the original vision and practices seems to have merit. This is evidenced in the Buddhist Forest Retreat Order, but also in forms of Christianity such as the Charismatic movement and the house churches. In each of these there is a significant evangelical element that opposes the norms of contemporary cultural values and is resistant to secularisation.

But there is a further element relating to conviction or faith, which seems to drive tradition and allow it to become relevant despite the processes of change. Above it was noted that role models were of importance if conversion was to occur or generational progression was to be achieved, for example, with Buddhist monks and nuns or within the family, with respect to parents. As a more extreme example we may note the way in which Hassidic Rebbes refused to leave their communities in the concentration camps, even when the option was made available to them. Here we are talking about the example of saints and martyrs, witnesses to the faith. This is at the heart of Shi'a Islam with the Imams Ali and Hussein. The revisitation of this example of conviction seems to be essential to the possibility of a tradition to renew itself, attract a new generation of followers, and inspire commitment in the young. This is, essentially, a standing against the encompassing values of a secularised world. It was the commitment and loyalty relied upon by both Stalin and Mao, it is the motivation of suicide bombers in Palestine and integral to understanding the events of September 11th in New York.

Whether this is a good thing, or a form of fanaticism, is another matter, but religious tradition seems to thrive on this conviction to bear witness (whether as the recipient of violence or as the perpetrator of the same) when it is under threat.

What is perceived to constitute this threat may vary but in the studies cited above the most obvious today is assimilation into an increasingly globalised secular culture. Neither ethnic nor national identity appear as a sufficient means of defence against this and thus what has been observed in relation to migrant communities can be said to apply equally to non-migrant ones. Conversion of the disaffected provides a spiritual regeneration of religious tradition, a means to its reconstruction; but to sustain it the next generation has to be convinced of its relevance to their aspirations when the promise and possibility of other things is on offer.

References

[1]   Orwell, G. 1984, *Animal Farm*, Harmondsworth, Penguin.

[2]   Narada, T. 1972, *The Dhammapada*, London, John Murray.

[3]   Sumedho, A. 1987, *Mindfulness: The Path to the Deathless*, Great Gaddesden, Herts, Amaravati Publications.

[4]   *When the Buddha Comes to Sussex* (transmission date 7 October 1979), London, BBC Publications.

[5]   Kashima, T. 1977, *Buddhism in America: the social organisation of an ethnic religious institution*, Greenwood Press

[6]   del Nevo, M. 1992, Letter from Lahore: Ozzy and Hussain, *The New Internationalist* 238, December.

[7]   Erricker, C. 2001, The Spiritual Education of Khoja Shia Ithnasheeri Youth: The Challenges of Diaspora in Erricjer, J., Ota, C. and Erricker, C. (eds) *Spiritual Education, Cultural, Religious and Social Differences: New Perspectives for the 21st Century*, Brighton, Academic Press.

[8]   Keysar, A., Kosmin, B. and Scheckner, J. 2000, *The Next Generation: Jewish Children and Adolescents*, Albany, State University of New York Press.

[9]   Winter, J. 1989, Income, Identity and Involvement in the Jewish Community: A Test of an Estimate of the Affordability of Living Jewishly, *Journal of Jewish Communal Service* 66(2),149-56.

LINKS IN A CHAIN: ANTIQUITY AND THE PRESENT IN BUILDING

Andrew Clegg

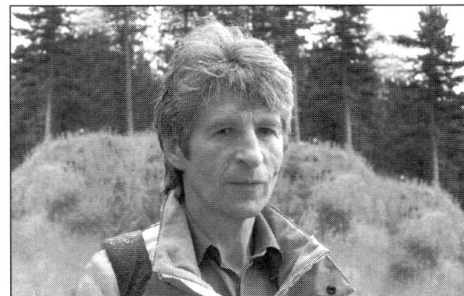

1. Introduction

Tradition, where the buildings on our Planet are concerned, is a summation of all things beautiful and useful, in materials and design. 'Things' that is, which have been 'handed on'... *tradere* is the Latin root of our word, meaning... *to hand on*.

I make no apology for the introduction of 'useful' as a criterion.

Buildings are required to be useful. Indeed, it is an imperative. Roofs and walls are wanted to keep us warm, when it is cold, and cool, when ambient temperatures are uncomfortably hot. Many of our building traditions are predicated on such simple premises, be it the inclusion of splashing water in the courtyard designs of the great buildings of the Caliphat of Cordoba or the huge wall constructions (solid stone walls) and spiral make-up so typical of the early Scots broch. The Moors, of course, required cooling: Scots needed more than whisky to keep them warm!

2. Traditional building materials

Moreover, there is a utilitarian undertow to a tradition in which the choice of materials is determined by their being '*traditionally*' available, which is to say, locally available. Materials, naturally, determine design. Thus, in the absence of much natural stone, and given the abundance of local clay in the flood plain of the Tigris and Euphrates rivers, brick was the natural choice of the peoples of Mesopotamia, among whom were builders – in Babylon, in particular – who owned the ability to make mud into a transcendent buildings material, of quite astonishing beauty.

ANDREW CLEGG

Andrew Clegg was educated at St Andrews University and has travelled widely in Europe, USA, Mexico, South America and North Africa. In 1994, together with two business partners Martin Deighton and Michael Challoner, he bought Scotland's oldest surviving brickworks at Errol in Perthshire (a brickworks whose earliest *recorded* production was in 1710 – although there are good grounds for dating its provenance to the pre Reformation late Medieval Period). Today the Errol Brick Company is a specialist brickmaker in the field of Conservation & Restoration. Andrew retired from day to day running of the Company in January 2005. Currently, he is chairman of STANZA (Scotland's International Poetry Festival) and a public speaker on several subjects: the Early Renaissance, European Poetry (Homer to Lorca), Brickmaking in the Ancient World, Arab Philosophers of the early Medieval Period and 19th century English and French poets and novelists. Andrew is a resident of Newburgh of Lindores, Scotland.

The tradition which *they* started, continues to flourish to the present day, as can be witnessed by any who travel in North Africa, or in the Middle East, owning an eye for the felicities and usefulness of ceramic masonry. The Berber brickmakers of Cobi and Taradoun, skilful in dried mud, are of a piece with the brickmakers of Nebuchadnezzar's time. For they are 'links in a chain.'

The sundering of that chain, world wide, has much to do with the introduction, on a large scale, of non-local building materials. Occasionally, there is a rationale, other than profit behind such movement, although pursuit of profit, more often than not, underscores the movement of materials. Any modern day traveller in Morocco, for example, cannot but be dismayed to behold the construction on the Atlantic coastal plain, in the area of Esouira, of a gigantic plant geared to the production of cement.

That cement production is said to account for some ten per cent of carbon emissions into the Earth's atmosphere is not the least cause for our dismay. That it should be compounded by the material's being utterly 'non traditional' and inimical to North Africa's built heritage, makes the introduction of such alien materials and techniques doubly disturbing.

Of course, in Morocco, as in other areas of the developing world, concrete is perceived to be a 'modern' material, whose use is a token of the region's aspirations to be part of the contemporary scheme of things. *Concreta* – as it happens – was a compound of aggregates and lime known to the Romans in the 1st Century BC, as ruinous remains and the writings of Vetruvius confirm. It might be said on that account to be a traditional building material, one lacking, however, in gravitas.

The Orcadian author, George Mackay Brown, writing in his novel 'Greenvoe' says '*All of the materials made by man grow graceful in time, except concrete.*' I'll second that! The catastrophic failure of reinforced concrete structures in those parts of the world subject to earthquakes, appears to hinder its progress not a jot! In this regard, it is worthy to note that traditional materials *with* gravitas, earth, mud, clay, are, if

Adam Williamson: Placing last stone-carved rosette onto gate, St Ethelberger Church, City of London. Photograph courtesy of John Allen, 2006.

not quite earthquake proof, better able to withstand seismic shock, on account of their natural flexibility. Concrete is unbending and rigid.

Common sense, derived from long term experience, often underpins the use of traditional materials.

This is only to emphasise what should be obvious. Building traditions in a particular locality are based upon what has been done before, and has been seen to be successful. The chain is so subtle that builders might not *know* why they are doing what they are doing. To a great extent, their lack of theory is frightening…or would be, if their buildings did not work. BUT THEY DO WORK.

'This is how we do it because this is how we've always done it: this is what we have been taught to do.'

So, journeymen handed on their experience to their apprentices, who having qualified in time as tradesmen, became journeymen in their own right, and handed on the skills which *they* had learned to a new generation of apprentices. No matter their trades, masons or carpenters, they are all 'links in a chain.'

It is not so long ago, of course, that such matters were highly formalised. The Guilds and such like Brotherhoods (Crafts & Trades) were committed to handing on skills in a manner, wholly based on understanding.

If the builders of '*Taigh Dhu*' for example, the Hebridean '*Black Houses*' with their thatched roofs and eccentric air flows might be said to be working blind, from the point of view of theory, the builders of Europe's great medieval cathedrals were anything but unconscious of what they were about.

Indeed, without a precise knowledge of lime technology, such massive structures could never have been put up to astonish both heaven and earth! No-one would claim that the Tirensians (who were the building arm of the Benedictine order) were unconscious of what they were about. Their grasp of theory was profound.

There were, however, many builders whom we could readily identify as being 'unconscious links.'

When was the last great cathedral constructed? I believe it was in the 1960s, in Medellin, Columbia, El Catedral del Cristo Rey, brick built and massive. Perhaps not quite a modern equivalent to Chartreuse or Notre Dame, but a worthy exercise in the tradition nonetheless.

In the field of eco-friendly construction techniques, struggling to be reborn in the northern hemisphere, (in the area of rammed earth building, for example, building in cob and wattle, unfired clay, call it what you will) the chain having been sundered, even in a couple of generations, builders are often at a loss how to proceed. There is no handbook to show us what to do, where to begin, how to continue. In short, the link is missing.

The question is, why have we, in the 'developed world' experienced such a diminution of the traditional skill pool, and why are we exporting techniques and materials to those parts of the 'un-developed' world, where traditional skills have flourished for thousands of years, effectively breaking the chain? In a word, well, there's no gain saying it, is there? Profit!

3. High margins! Profit!

Returning to the tradition of Nebuchadnezzar and brick making and building skills communicated *via* Alexander the Great to the peoples of the eastern Mediterranean and thence to the Romans and their imperial domain in northern Europe, we can say that margins were always modest, where mud was concerned, chiefly on account of its being in plentiful supply in the flood plains of Europe's great rivers. In other words, no great effort was required and no merchant traders were involved in sourcing the required material.

This is not to say that merchant involvement in sourcing far flung materials is a bad thing *per se* witness Nebuchadnezzar's use of cedar wood for temple building and his builders' sourcing of materials for the glazing of brickwork, only that the primary material, traditionally, was of local provenance, and, consequently, inexpensively won. Where locally available materials are concerned,

Malca Schotten: Flint Knapper III – study in grey and yellow, Brandon, Suffolk 2004, pastel, charcoal, pigment on painted paper, 154cm x 75.5cm. Reproduced by permission of the artist.

Martin Shortis, Sutton House Repairing.
Reproduced by permission of the artist.

to knock such common sense on the head, in the interest of profit, is thoroughly wrong headed and perverse.

4. The most ancient and traditional trade on earth

Let us examine, in a little more detail, the *positive* consequences of our maintaining our links with what has gone before.

The brickmaker's is the most ancient and most traditional trade of all. The earliest brick built structure found on Earth, dates back to the 13th millennium *before* the Christian era.

Thermo-luminescence has dated this building, near Thebes on the upper Nile, to that long-gone age and even if it is a simple structure

Richard Kindersley: Public Arts Commission for Midland Railway town of Wolverton. The relief is 2 x4 metres long and shows the classic configuration of the main drive wheels and connecting rods of steam locomotives.

Malca Schotten: Making clay lump, study I, Spooner Row, Norfolk 2002, charcoal on paper, 70cm x 100cm. Reproduced by permission of the artist.

created out of bricks of caked mud, it shows us a trade, the brickmaker's trade, of considerable antiquity.

The link, however, remains intact: the chain that begins its loop 15,000 years ago, and takes in brickmakers on the Nile, from Potiphar's and Neftari's day, brickmakers on the shores of Mesopotamia's rivers, from the time of King Nebopolassar & King Nubuchadnezzar, kings *and* bricklayers. Greek and Etruscan brickmakers, who were encouraged in their trade by Alexander the Great and those builders in clay, who accompanied the Roman Legions from the Rhine and Cisalpine Gaul, all over the known world that chain loops around me and my colleagues today. Together, we *are* links in that ancient chain.

We derive a good deal of encouragement from the fact! Necessary encouragement and welcome, since, without a vestige of a doubt, ours is a dwindling business, both in terms of our market and our operations. Brick's share of the former has been shrinking, for more than a generation, and the number employed in the Brick Industry, once legion, has been reduced to a rump.

Some would say that the draughtsman's skills in detailing brickwork are also becoming a thing of the past – another link sundered. Without imaginative detailing, perhaps, without even the basic mathematical skills wanted in brick stretcher bond, how many metric units to the square metre? Well, let's just go for prefabricated panels – o tempora, o mores!

I dread to think what would be built were there a couple of Pharoes around today, wanting to be buried! 'Anybody know anything about limestone cladding of a mud brick triangle?'

Of course, brickmakers have seen off competition, in many forms, for many thousands of years and will shrug off the present decline in a more or less casual manner, to win through once more.

History enables us to say so, with complete confidence.

The availability of limestone, to clad the pyramids, didn't stop bricks being built in ancient Egypt, where they are used to this day.

The popularity of products from the Trabertine Quarries (the poor man's marble) failed to put a stop to brickmaking on the Tiber's shores. In our own day, Italy is among the world's leading, and most innovative, brickmaking nations.

The marble and limestone that was available to the Greeks, from the time of Phideas onwards, didn't mean a cessation of brick building in the Levant.

For a thousand years, however, from the demise of Rome's empire, to the re-discovery of the brickmaker's art, in the 13th Century, by Dutch craftsmen, no bricks of fired earth were produced in the northern parts of the old Empire. None!

Today, Germany, Austria, Holland and France are amongst the most prolific and technically advanced of brickmakers. Even so, contemporary skills fall far short of the creative abilities of brickmakers of Mesopotamia, three thousand years ago. At least, contemporary outlets for such skills are rare and seldom.

One need look only towards the *Ishtar Gate* and *Processional Way* in Babylon, to see how things once were. Those silvered and glazed *Sirrush* (beautiful beyond measure) and yellow lions, red haired, in bas relief brickwork, so exquisitely tricked out in burned and enamelled clay, take our breath away today.

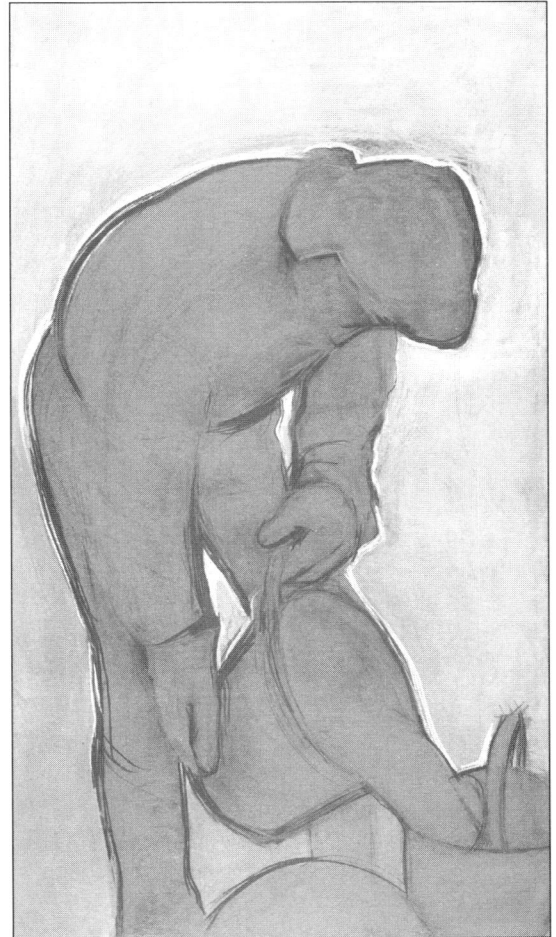

Malca Schotten: Making clay lump I, Spooner Row, Norfolk 2004, charcoal, pigment, pastel on paper, 215cm x 100cm. Reproduced by permission of the artist.

Richard Kindersley: Public Arts Commission in Ely. The carving shows the miracle of the Saint's staff taking root and sprouting leaves. 1800 x 2650. St Etheldreda was founder and first Abbess of Ely Cathedral.

Our own marvels in terracotta – chiefly from the Victorian and Edwardian eras, include St Pancras Station or High Holbourne's temple to Insurance Brokerage or Templeton's Carpet Warehouse on Glasgow Green, with its arabesque chevron patterns, or Glasgow Port Authority's 'Tower of the Winds' (derived from an Athenian model) or any one of a half dozen period structures in Birmingham or the occasional Oxford College and so on and so forth.

Our own marvels, I say – are as nothing when compared with the glorious brickwork of King Nebuchadnezzar's era.

Not that the chain is altogether broken. Our own company – Errol Brick Company – undertook a commission a couple of years ago, to provide a larger than life footballer in carved brickwork, prepared precisely in the identical manner of Babylon. Its execution was a joy to behold. Our client was a provincial football club!

I recall, when the artist was working on her mud bricked elevation on a reinforced easel in our 'Beehive Kiln' I began to read out to her, standing behind her, notes from Professor Koldeway's painstaking exposition of how 'bas relief' brickwork was achieved in Ancient Babylon. As detailed a breakdown of the technique as you could imagine, when, not looking around, the artist said to me, 'I didn't think I'd written any of that down.'

That was marvellous. The link with the ceramic artistry of Nebuchadnezzar's glorious city had been re-created, as it were, out of pure fancy and imagination, coupled with the artist's sense of good practice. Now THAT was encouraging.

Naturally, in almost every other part of the globe, wherever clays are available, brick is the first choice for building, either in its un-fired form as 'adobe' or 'earth' brick or, burned in a bewildering variety of kilns, in its more customary 'hard based' form.

Like bread from wheaten flour, bricks of clay endure. And as the baker, so the brickmaker.

Sometimes we can mistake the importance of a tradition (be quite blind to it, indeed) when, for example, the traditional material isn't primary. Scotland is a case in point. Scotland's first and most important material was natural stone. There was plenty of it.

Go about the land and its evidence is all around: the red and black whinstones of Balmullo, in Fife; the yellow limestone of Craigleith's quarry, in the Lothians, a stone which gives Edinburgh's New Town its distinctive character; the russet sandstone of Dumfries and Galloway; the silver granite of Aberdeen; the pink *ditto* of the Pentland Firth.

All these areas, traditionally, reflected their own sourced material, to such an extent that anyone with a knowledge of local building traditions could be taken to a location, in a manner, blindfolded, and once un-blinded, could tell at a glance *where* they were. Stone is no longer quarried, generally speaking, and with the arrival of 'reconstituted stone products' – which is to say, concrete products with handfuls of stone dust thrown into the mix, all of this local character has vanished from our new buildings. Everywhere is rapidly becoming everywhere else – with all that *that* entails for our sense of place and civic identity.

The oldest fired brick building discovered in Scotland dates back to Roman times. The bath houses at the Roman Fort at Inchtuthill, at the confluence of the Rivers Tay and Isla, were built in clay bricks produced on the spot, making use, incidentally, of the same clay source as people use today.

You will readily imagine how proud that makes people feel, to be working in a tradition established in Scotland, by the brickmakers, attached to the legions of Julius Agricola...the glorious *Augusta and Victorix!* Making use of the same source material as Roman brickmakers nearly 2,000 years ago, is as fine an example of linkage as can possibly be imagined.

5. Conclusion

In conclusion, a link connectes the ancient past, to which the Romans were linked before now, and the Greeks before *them* and prior to the period of Pericles' Athens, so the links go on, back to Babylon, to the time of Hamurabi and Zargon, to the glory days of Ur and Somer, all the way back to that humble hut on the Nile, constructed out of baked earth.

I am confident, beyond telling, that our line will continue until doomsday, and for all I know to the contrary, beyond.

Law,
Legibility
&
Language

Ancient Letter Carving And Computer Type Design

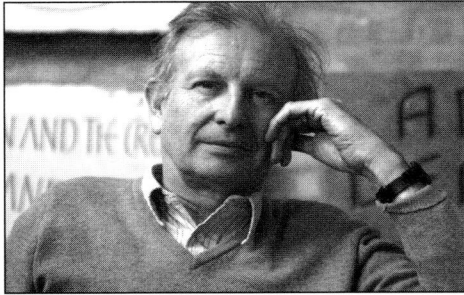

Richard Kindersley

Richard Kindersley

Richard studied lettering at his father's Studio in Cambridge and Sculpture at Cambridge School of Art. His lettering is to be found on buildings throughout the country. For his contribution to architectural lettering and inscriptions he was awarded an Honorary Fellowship of the Royal Institute of British Architects as well as The Royal Society for Arts Award for Art in Architecture.

Commissions for The National Museum of Scotland, the National Gallery of Ireland, Dublin, The Public Records Office Kew, Main entrance to Keele University. Group of 10 Standings Stones for the Pilgrims Way. Group of 8 Standing Stones commissioned by BP International for their new headquarters. The British 9/11 Memorial, Grosvenor Square. Major public art inscription for the Jubilee line.

He has developed over recent years a passion for Standing Stones, reformulating them for our own times. This has produced a genuine response from the public with commissions from across the UK and several in the USA.

1. Introduction

Why, at the beginning of the 21st century, am I still carving letters by hand in stone? There are a number of answers, ranging from the childhood delight in carving one's initials into the trunks of trees to the adult pleasure of simply making permanent fine marks on stone. There is, however, a more relevant and interesting connection that binds our modern world to this most ancient way of leaving a trace of our existence.

2. Trajan and Gladiator

People who stand in front of Trajan's Column in Rome, marvel at the wonderfully detailed relief carving that spirals down the pillar, recording the battles and victories of The Emperor Trajan. But those of us interested in lettering will look at the marble panel at the base of the column. It was carved in about 112AD and contains exquisitely carved letters representing the high point in the development of the Imperial Roman inscriptions. The letter forms, which are highly sophisticated, beautifully drawn and cut with great authority, epitomize the state, power and majesty of Imperial Rome.

The forms are driven, however, by the more modest action of the pen and brush giving the characteristic thick and thin letters strokes.

If we move forward to the 20th–21st century we discover a reincarnation of the Trajan column letters. In 1989 Carol Twomby, then an employee of Adobe Systems, drew an alphabet based closely on the Trajan inscription.

Be still.

Trajan's Column.

Adam Williamson: Artist carving memorial for Queen Elizabeth II. Photograph courtesy of Peter Saunders, 2005.

Although initially designed as simply a digitising exercise, the beauty and economy of the letter forms encouraged Adobe to issue it as a commercial font, aptly named Trajan. The font has been a runaway success ranging in use from newspaper headlines to ubiquitous application in film advertising.

TRAJAN

GLADIATOR

These beautiful Roman letters designed almost 20 centuries ago have been transported to the digital age and democratised for us all to use and enjoy.

3. New typefaces

The process of producing a new typeface is to draw with pencil the individual letters and then scan them into one of the powerful type design programs. The drawing is fine tuned on screen, adjusted for digitising and the letter spacing parameters introduced. Working from these early Roman models the Trajan typeface has built into it the natural order of aesthetics deriving from the mind, hand and eye working in concert.

With the superficial ease of computer type design there is a glut of gimmicky fonts around as anybody will know if they look at the free typefaces that came with their computer. In spite of much inappropriate design there are a few designers whose background is both calligraphy and drawn letters who are producing beautiful and practical type designs. Their designs are therefore infused with the tradition and tools of craft in addition to employing the new tools of our age. The special quality of their designs comes from the discipline of hand lettering and the use of traditional tools that imparts a rhythm and structure into the letter that appeals to the eye and draws the mind to their harmony.

The acknowledged master of this approach to type design is the German Herman Zapf. Many readers will be familiar with his type although not necessarily his name. These designs include Palatino, Optima and Michelangelo.

PALATINO

MICHELANGELO

Richard Kindersley: carved Welsh Slate inscription on permanent display in the gallery of the 20th Century at the V & A Museum, London. The inscription set out in a spiral is a quotation from one of Ruskin's lectures.

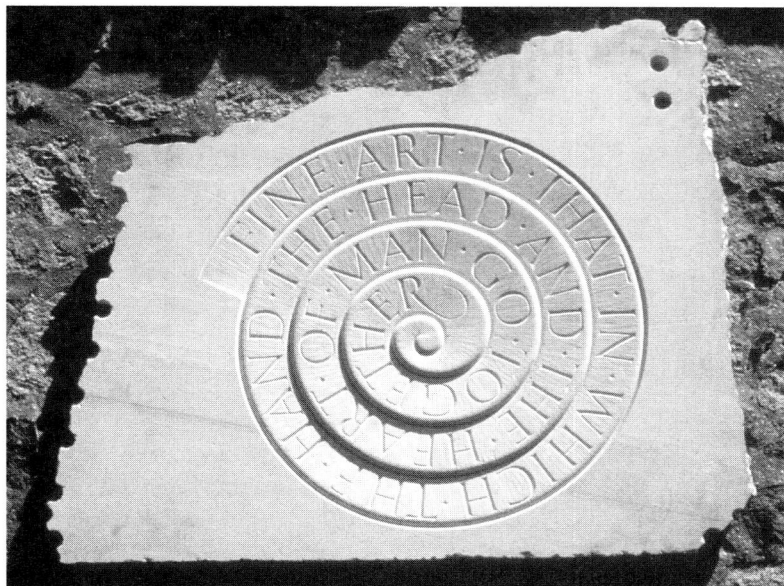

Fine Art inscription, carved Portland Stone.

Contemporary designers such as Michael Harvey and Jason Smith all acknowledge that the most successful type designs come from a combination of drawing and computer skills. The drawing comes first. Jason Smith, a young designer producing corporate faces including the new designs for the Post Office, gave an illuminating example at a conference last year. He explained that when he left Reigate College of Art, fuelled up with a belief in computer design and the over arching confidence of youth, he was accepted into the Monotype drawing office. A feather in his cap. To his horror, he was instructed during his first day at Monotype to simply draw freehand with a pencil as near perfect circles as he could. He felt initially insulted but on reflection he quickly saw the point. To look, to see and to understand. To enable through the act of drawing a circle to train the eye, hand and mind. It is almost platonic in its simplicity. This lesson in drawing so clearly evident in the classical Roman inscriptions is still pertinent today in designing the best electronic typefaces.

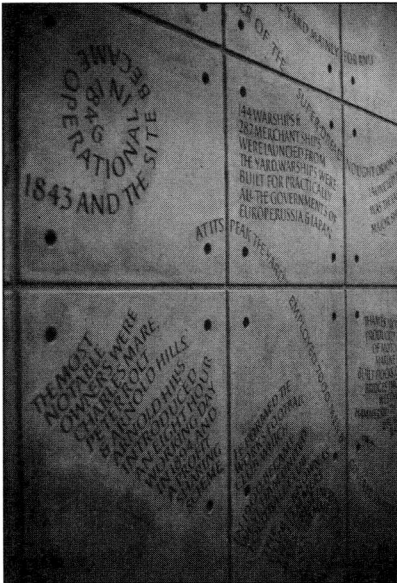

Richard Kindersley: Detail of Public Arts Commission for Canning Town Underground Station on the new Jubilee Line.

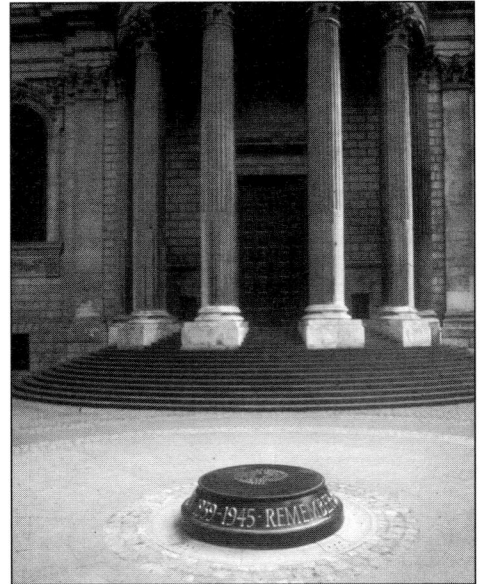

Richard Kindersley: St Paul Cathedral memorial to the people of London who died in the blitz 1939–1945. The memorial is carved from a three ton block of Irish limestone.

4. Conclusion

Although I design with the computer, my main work is carving inscriptions in stone. My question to the reader is why? My answer is that the joy in seeing Roman inscriptions is not founded in antiquity, but it is in the seeing of objects that are made by hand, we have a hunger for things handmade, to touch and explore through our senses fine objects made by others.

They become a sounding board transmitting an essentially human aspect of spirit. This is not a luxury but a necessity, a food for enriching our lives. The more we surround ourselves with the machine made, the mechanical reproduction, the more we need to occasionally touch and see objects made by hand, to retrace with eye and hand the care and vision of the maker. The traditional craft of lettering is required both in the high-tech world of type design but also for our need for visual nourishment.

Richard Kindersley:
Carved vertical sundial with gilded sun design.

LANGUAGE AS TRADITION

Viktor Zhivov

VICTOR ZHIVOV

Viktor Zhivov was born in Moscow, Russia in 1945. He is professor of the Department of Slavic Languages and Literatures at the University of California at Berkeley and deputy director of the Institute of the Russian Language of the Russian Academy of Sciences (Moscow). His main areas of study are general and Slavic linguistics, language typology, Russian and Byzantine cultural history. His main publications include: 'Aspects of Syntagmatic Phonology' (1980); 'Language and Culture of Russia of the Eighteenth Century' (1996); 'Studies on the History and Prehistory of the Russian Culture' (2002); 'Chapters on Historical Morphology of the Russian Language in the Seventeenth and Eighteenth Centuries' (2004); 'Studies on Church History in the Time of Peter the Great' (2004).

1. Introduction

For the last century, language has been regarded primarily as a phenomenon belonging to the sphere of nature rather than to the sphere of culture. This great divide of nature and culture is not so clearly drawn now as it was half a century ago but the opposition still holds. In particular, there are laws in nature but traditions in culture. A free falling body falls with a certain acceleration quite independently of its individual qualities, without regard for its willingness or reluctance to perform the act of falling, its perception of gravity and other similar factors. The same can be said about living creatures. Birds sing their wedding songs not because they try to woo the love and affection of their potential mates, but because they reproduce an inherited habit; they have no choice, their behaviour is genetically determined. It is different with humans. We also do a lot of things habitually, without any reflection, our manners of eating, greeting each other and so on are largely automatic. However, even with most automatic manners, there is a possibility of choice. We can decide to behave like a 'barbarian' or to greet our friends with a special gesture. Consequently, we reproduce our habits not by instinct, but by tradition. We reproduce them in accordance with our national, class, or local identity and we perceive these habits, at least implicitly, as manifestations of our identity. They are elements of our culture, not of our nature.

2. Structuralist approach

One can see now what is meant by association of language with the sphere of nature. Language is conceptualized as an organic structure, as a natural phenomenon, which is by no means governed by human reflection. The great founder of structuralism in linguistics, Ferdinand de Saussure, taught that language was a system in which all elements were related to each other and each element was defined exclusively by its relationships to all the other elements. In the view of de Saussure and other structuralists, language turns out to be a fairly complicated and tightly knit system with a multitude of internal dependencies and at the same time with no external dependencies at all. You can ask how that could be, in light of the fact that language is involved in human communication, which, in its turn, depends on cultural, social, and historical circumstances. Saussure solved this problem by opposing language to speech. Speech is immersed in real life and external factors exert on it an easily perceptible influence, but it is generated by language, by an abstract mechanism which is totally unconnected with the circumstances of communication. Ostensibly, this mechanism resides in the human brain, but otherwise it has nothing human in it; it is rather like an algebraic structure or, as Saussure himself said, like chess. It is placed into human beings as a monolithic block; they can certainly use it for their own benefit; it is used as the instrument of verbal communication, but it is used much in the same way as stars are used to navigate.

3. Language and change

There are advantages in this approach; it has provided for the progress of linguistics during the last century, theoretical grammar of Noam Chomsky and his followers has been constructed on this basis and many important discoveries have been made. I will discuss instead its disadvantages. From our perspective, the main one is that it utterly destroys the subject of this paper. If language were an algebraic structure

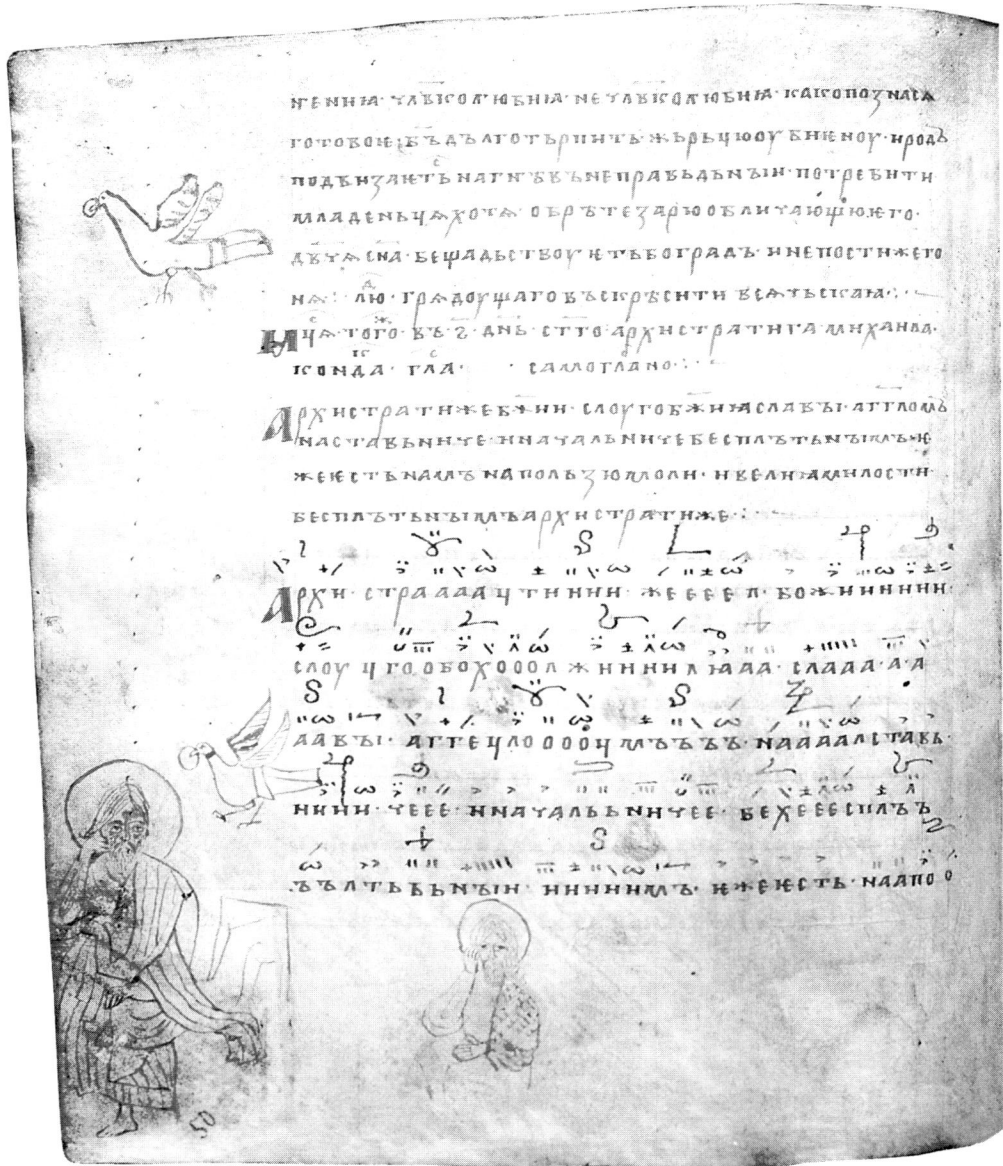

Tipografskii ustav (The Printing House Monastic Rule), Slavonic manuscript of the late 11th – early 12th centuries, containing a translation of the Studion monastic rule and a kontakarion (church hymns with special musical notation), fol.25 versus. The manuscript is in State Tretiakov Gallery, Moscow, no.K-5349. The facsimile is published as: Tipografskii ustav. Ustav s kondakarem kontsa XI – nachala XII veka. Ed. by B.A. Uspenskii. Vol.I. Moscow, Iazyki slavianskikh kul'tur, 2006. Reproduced with permission.

of sorts, it would have nothing to do with traditions. But it is not true, language is as much influenced by traditions as any other human institution or, in other words, it is as much made up of traditions as any social phenomenon existing in history. There is no history in Saussurean linguistics and this is its crucial drawback. Language, as we know it, is in the constant process of change. Saussurean linguistics cannot explain change; it relegates change to the sphere of speech, but this stratagem does not help because change affects the mechanism itself, not only the results of its functioning. If language is an algebraic structure, it has no reason to change; algebraic structures do not change even when they are in the service of human beings.

There is one further complication. Confronted with the task of describing linguistic change, structuralist linguistics has to treat it as a sudden instantaneous process, as a disaster. You will recall that for Saussure and other structuralists, language is defined as a system in which all elements are connected and circumscribed solely by their connections with all other elements. If this were the case, the change of any one element would be simultaneously the change of the whole system. Any change would be a change of a structural principle, of basic rules, made in one leap. However, we know from experience that changes in linguistic usage are incremental. We know, for instance, that using the adjective *cute* in the sense of 'pretty' or 'clever' is a relatively recent innovation, it still sounds informal and juvenile, but it has gained ground during our lifetime. Late Latin still had case declension which was subsequently lost in French. We can justifiably treat this loss as a change of a structural principle, but there was a period of several centuries when this change was in transition. It proceeded from one class of words to another, it expanded from informal speech genres to more formal; from generation to generation it was adopted by one social group after another. At any given moment during this transition, there existed in the language competing structural principles distributed over a wide range of social, cultural, and stylistic usages. From a strict structuralist point of view, there was no language at all. Well, Structuralism has invented a number of rather artificial stratagems to tackle this problem, but this does not concern us here. What is important here is the fact that the retention of old variants was due to tradition, to the desire of speakers to preserve inherited elements of their language; this desire was grounded in their cultural, social, and stylistic predilections.

Thus, linguistic change involves social, cultural, and historical factors; it is based on imitation and the decision to imitate. In general terms, linguistic change proceeds on a generational basis. Members of a younger generation imitate the speech of their parents, and in turn transmit their linguistic habits to their children. They construct their own grammar (their patterns of usage) taking as their starting point the speech they hear in their social and cultural environment (especially during their childhood and adolescent years). Their reconstruction may differ in a number of points from the grammar of the preceding generation: reconstructions usually do not coincide with their models in every detail. These differences constitute change. In some cases a series of changes proceeds in the same direction; from generation to generation separate instances of the same change accumulate and bring the change of a structural principle. In other cases there is no regularity in a generational progression of changes and no change of a structural principle is obtained. The result depends on the speakers. Change is human; it is not predetermined by structural principles or other elemental forces. It is effected by a long row of reinterpretations of a traditional usage produced by succeeding generations. Their choice is not governed by structural principles; it depends on their will, on their desire, on their efforts to imitate their seniors and to preserve their identity.

4. Arbitrariness of change: an example

A random example is the extension of 'intrusive linking /r/' in American English. In the original coastal dialects of American English, /r/ not followed by a vowel was de-rhotacized to [ə]. Examples are *ear* [iə] [diə], *poor* [puə]. (An analogous change occurs in many dialects of English in England proper.) In the northern half of the dialects, from

Martin Shortis, Merevale Renovation.
Reproduced by permission of the artist.

New York to Boston, this vocoid [ə̣] was absorbed if the preceding vowel was a low vowel. Thus in the northern dialects, in place of general American *care*, we have [kæ], instead of the general American pronunciation in the preposition *for*, in these dialects we hear [fɔ]. This change has not taken place in position before a vowel. There, the original /r/ was generally preserved as a link with a following word beginning with a vowel: the phrase *care of* is pronounced [kærʌv], the phrase *for a while* retains the consonant [fɔrə], two kinds of vehicles is *car and truck* [kar ənd črʌk], and the phrase *father alone* is pronounced as [faðərəlon]. As a result, words with the original final /r/ would have two variants, one with a final low vowel and another with the final /r/.

The 'intrusive linking /r/' is the extension of this pattern. The dialectologists describe it as follows: 'On the basis of such doublets… positional allomorphs [morphological variants] ending in /r/ are often created in Eastern New England and Metropolitan New York for words that historically end in the vowels /ɔ, a, ə/, as *law, ma, Martha*' [1]. This usage is an extension of the previous one because originally these words did not end in /r/. Regardless of this fact, now 'one hears *law and order* /lɔr ənd ɔdə/, *ma and pa* /mar ən(d) pa/, *Martha and I* /maθər ənd ai/.' That is, one hears a consonant /r/ pronounced between one of these words and a closely linked following word that begins with a vowel, when these words never contained any consonant /r/.

In this way a new pattern was created out of the old one; one pattern of usage in certain words was taken as a model for developing analogous patterns in other words that ended in similar vowels. The new pattern is a curious one; its peculiarity consists in the fact it is activated only after the low vowels. The dialectologists highlight this peculiarity: 'It is worth noting that after the normally up-gliding free vowels /i, u, e, o/, as in *three, two, day, know,* an analogical "intrusive" /r/ never occurs. The reason for this is clear: since /θri, tu, de, no/ do not end like the phrase-final /r/-less allomorphs of *ear, poor, care, four* /iə̯, puə̯, keə̯, foə̯/, the basis for creating allomorphs ending in /r/ is lacking.' What is striking about this pattern is that it is not governed by a structural principle. Low vowels as a class of sounds that trigger the intrusive /r/ constitute only a semblance of a structural factor because nothing on earth sets them apart from other vowels as specially propitious for intrusive sounds. The reason why low vowels are the environment in the extension of intrusive /r/ is solely because this is the set of vowels that had already absorbed the vocoid [ə̯] and thereby provided the model for intrusive /r/.

5. Language and cultural identity

It can be said that the resulting usage preserves the memory of its ancestors, of the usage of previous generations; in this sense it is traditional. It is shaped by tradition and by the desire to maintain this tradition, not by structural principles. Language is a playground of cultural identities. Speech is not generated by a mysterious *automaton;* it is produced by human beings who at every instance habitually indicate their attitude toward cultural dimensions of their pronouncements. They do it by imitating a set of culturally defined modes of speech. At one moment a speaker tries to sound Shakespearean and insert a tacit allusion in his or her turn of a phrase, at another he or she mimics a schoolteacher, and so on and so forth.

One could conceivably raise an objection to this thesis and argue that in most cases our speech is neutral, that usually we want only to convey information without showing any personal attitude. However, neutrality is an ambiguous notion. What sounds neutral to one person turns out to be peculiar in the perception of another. Everyone probably can remember instances of social misunderstanding when one is shocked by the preciosity or vulgarity of one's interlocutor whereas this interlocutor is absolutely unconscious of any irregularity in his or her speech and considers it neutral. In the last analysis, neutrality presupposes tradition. We regard as neutral those forms of speech which correspond to traditions inherited by us from the preceding generation and accepted by our social environment. I would like to remind you of Major Pendennis, an elderly beau from William Thackeray's novel *Pendennis*. He said to his nephew who wanted to marry a provincial actress: 'Fancy your wife attached to a mother who dropped her *h*'s, or called Maria Marire!' This poor lady thought that her speech was neutral.

6. Written language

To this point I have in effect been discussing only oral language. It would be impossible to discuss traditions in language and confine the discussion to the oral form of language. I will not meddle with Jacques Derrida's famous thesis, according to which the written form of language is the primary one, a position that seems to ignore the fact that language was spoken for millennia before the invention of writing. I would like, however, to draw your attention to the fact that written and spoken languages are two very different phenomena. Their difference is not limited to their external form, or – to use a scholarly expression – to the nature of their signifiers: sounds in one case and letters or hieroglyphs in the other. From the structuralist point of view, this difference is of little importance. The only purpose of signifiers is to serve as distinctive features that make it possible to differentiate semantic units. In this respect it is irrelevant whether they are made of sounds, letters, the long and short signals of the Morse codes or Braille signs, in the same way as it is irrelevant whether chessmen are made of wood, ivory, or porcelain.

But in fact, I would argue, it makes all the difference. Written texts can be read over and over whereas oral texts exist only as long as they are pronounced. As a consequence, oral speech and written texts are structured differently. Complex sentences are rather an exception in oral speech; they never occur in dialogues, which, after all, is the main form of oral communication. One can hardly imagine a Proustian period even in a very refined conversation. On the contrary, long sentences look natural in written texts. In general, producers of oral and written texts employ different syntactic strategies. A fact that may not be self-evident is that one needs different sets of grammatical elements to construct written and oral texts. Complicated embedded predicates such as various participle, gerund or infinitive constructions are out of place in a dialogue. It may be claimed that oral and written languages have different grammars. Even if the elements are the same their functions are different. In many languages participles play different roles or, in other words, have different meaning in written and oral production.

These different grammatical structures correspond to different ways in which oral and written texts are learned. It is much easier to preserve and to transmit information in written form than orally. The network of memory as a social institution in literate societies is not identical to the structure of inherited information in societies which manage their traditions without the recourse to writing. Socrates in Plato's *Timeus* speaks with regret about the invention of writing because according to him it means the death of memory. If texts can be written down there is no need to learn them by heart. The ancient tradition of the art of memory, as it was called by Frances Yates, is falling apart [2]. Socrates was partly right. The invention of writing brought disaster to ancient ritualistic memory and to the ancient hieratic culture that is tightly connected with it. Indeed, ancient mnemonic techniques made it possible to maintain certain religious traditions, but at the same time restricted the variety of information that could be preserved by a society as its cultural heritage. The invention of writing put an end to this limitation. Written culture is able to maintain a multiplicity of traditions; written language is the most important means of their transmission and development.

7. Continuity and artificiality in written language

Actually, written language is mastered as a language of tradition *par excellence*, and it is used in traditional ways after being mastered. Writing is immersed in a cultural continuity. We write as we were taught to write, taught not only in school but also by the whole network of cultural institutions of our society. We shape our thoughts in the ways that have been prescribed by traditional genres of writing, and we use linguistic elements in configurations that have been conventionalized for a certain genre. A French writer – whether a famous maitre or a simple schoolboy – cannot narrate a story without using the *passé simple* even though this tense would be out of place in his oral speech. Certain grammatical forms and constructions are inevitable in any written exposition even if they are rare or impossible in speech. It means that they are used by tradition, as conventional features of certain genres of writing.

Because these features are conventional, they are often called artificial, but artificiality again is a deceptive concept. If some linguistic elements are artificial, then other linguistic elements are natural. Artificiality of one set of elements presupposes naturalness of another. This concept brings us back to the representation of language as a natural phenomenon. We already know that this view of language is one-sided. It is untrue both with respect to spoken language and with respect to written language, but its erroneousness is more evident in the latter case than in the former. What would it mean to say that language is artificial? It would mean that language is a system in itself, that normally people use language as they use their ability to see or to hear, and that any intrusion of human will or human art into the domain of this 'natural' ability is similar to such artificial contrivances as spectacles or hearing aids. Following this line of thinking, one would have to say that it is artificial when French schoolchildren use the *passé simple*; it does not come from their natural ability but is manufactured for them by their teachers.

This argument is essentially wrong because, as we know, any linguistic activity consists of the reproduction and combination of inherited elements, of elements that have been prepared, one might say, by preceding generations. The putative naturalness of the spoken language, its supposed primacy in comparison with the written language, is fictitious. In this respect written language does not significantly differ from spoken language. We do not write as we speak, we write as we read. Our writing habits are based on our reading experience. French schoolchildren use the *passé simple* in their written compositions not because they are taught by their instructors to do so, but because they know from many texts which they mastered that this is the way in which written texts should be composed.

Let me further expand on this point. Written language is often regarded as in some way a derivative of spoken language. The main, seemingly irrefutable, argument is based on the fact that there are (or there were) societies which do not possess any writing system; there are languages that exist only in the spoken form but not vice versa. There certainly are a number of dead languages, but we presume that there once existed a society that used these languages as means of oral communication. It is true, but this argument deals with historical origins and disregards linguistic diversity in well-developed societies.

In societies with traditional literacy, written languages are largely independent of spoken languages, both in their functioning and in their development. They constitute a separate or autonomous tradition. This tradition is based on the fact, mentioned earlier, that people write as they read. There is the same progress and the same continuity of linguistic competence from generation to generation as we have already observed in discussing linguistic history. Two lines, one of the spoken language and one of the written language, run parallel and sometimes interact in their developments, but they remain lines that are in principle separate. One special feature of this transmission ought to be mentioned in this connection. In the case of spoken languages, the transmission of linguistic competence is carried out on a strictly generational basis. We imitate the speech of our parents, not the speech of our great grandparents whom in ordinary circumstances we have never met. In the case of written languages, we imitate a body of heterogeneous texts, which we have read during our life. This body usually comprises texts composed in different epochs, often long before our own lifetime. At least that was the case for many centuries when an average literate person used to assimilate cultural achievements of the past and did not read only verbal stuff recently placed on an Internet site. Perhaps, as my colleague Manuel Castells argues [3], we are present at the birth of a new civilization in which my ideas about the written culture won't hold anymore, but the future is unpredictable and we won't attempt to discuss it here.

8. Modern standard language and registers

Let us go instead into the past. We are accustomed to a situation in which our written language is more or less uniform; it does not depend significantly on the genre of writing or on the subject of our composition. The language is the same at least in its main orthographic, morphological, and syntactic traits. However, a standard language is a feature of modernity. In pre-modern and early modern times the situation was different. Each genre of writing had its own linguistic peculiarities or, in other words, maintained its own linguistic tradition. This linguistic diversity is easily explainable. We know that writing habits are based on reading experience. Now, in a medieval society different sectors of the literate population read different texts. One can say, simplifying somewhat, that monks read their monastic rules and theological treatises, courtiers read their novels of adventure and collections of love songs, and chancellery officials and lawyers perused

Martin Shortis, Grand Buildings, Trafalgar Square. Reproduced by permission of the artist.

various official documents and legal codes. As a consequence, these various individuals were in possession of different types of reading experience. As a consequence, they reproduced different modes of writing pertinent to specific cultural traditions.

This last point has interesting repercussions. It means that the variety of writing traditions in a given society reflects its cultural and social divisions. We can get a glimpse of how a society is structured by studying and classifying linguistic features of the texts that were produced in a given epoch. In other words, we can establish how many distinct cultural traditions were maintained by a society, how they interacted and how they constructed a spectrum of social and cultural identities. Language is an excellent mirror; thanks to it we are able to take a look at a society from the inside.

Let me discuss a simple example. In England in the seventeenth century the press flourished (comparatively speaking). Numerous newspapers and innumerable pamphlets and leaflets were published. As a result, journalism became institutionalized and its language formed a distinct discourse of sorts. It had its own syntactic peculiarities (especially in headings), its favorite turns of phrase, and so on. It is possible to claim that it constituted a separate tradition of writing. In Muscovy of the same period there was only one newspaper, which was produced in a manuscript form (though book publishing existed and religious service books and other religious texts were published regularly). This newspaper was produced in one copy only, for the benefit of the tsar and his counselors. It appeared at irregular intervals and consisted of translations from various West European sources. The translations were made by officials of the Foreign Chancellery. The language of these translations is an extension of the Russian chancellery language, reproducing its specific morphology, syntactic patterns and lexical make-up.

Linguistic evidence is quite revealing. I do not mean the well known fact that Muscovy in the seventeenth century was an underdeveloped backward country in comparison with England or the Netherlands or France, a country where, in the words of Samuel Collins, tsar Aleksei

Mikhailovich's court physician, 'they being wholly devoted to their own Ignorance […] look upon Learning as a Monster.'[4] He was rather unjust in his estimation, as can be inferred from the fact that they did in fact translate foreign news and invite foreign physicians. But we need not go into that here. What is interesting about linguistic features is that they reveal not only the actual state of affairs, which can be easily learned from other sources, but also the state of the mind or, to be more precise, the state of the cultural consciousness. In contrast to Englishmen of the period, Muscovites did not regard journalism as a special kind of cultural activity; they did not associate it with literary pursuits (since literary texts were written in a different language), but regarded it rather as a sort of bureaucratic operation. This conception of journalism tells us a lot about the perception of culture, about the limitations that were imposed on the cultural domain, and about the relationships between state and society.

I would not say that there is only one writing tradition in modern societies, but there is no doubt that in pre-modern societies the differences between various traditions of writing (or registers, as they are called in linguistic studies) were more pronounced, the boundaries more sharply defined, and changes are more noticeable. What is especially important is that medieval and early modern texts are the best material to study how various traditions interact. I have in

Oxford Circus. Reproduced by permission of The Prince's Drawing School.

mind those phenomena that I mentioned earlier. Traditions interact in the linguistic activity of individual speakers or writers. Usually a writer followed a certain tradition of writing in accordance with his professional calling and appropriate reading experience and in accordance with the subject matter of his composition. However, he was not obliged to follow this tradition slavishly. As a rule, he was cognizant of other traditions and could pick up some linguistic elements belonging to these other traditions and insert them in his text.

He could do that for various reasons. In some cases it was done because the author did not know how to formulate the intended message with the means provided by his primary tradition. We can imagine, for instance, that a chronicler writing about a legal dispute might borrow characteristic constructions and expressions from legal discourse. In other and more interesting cases it was done on purpose to mark the whole text or some passage from it as something special, as something overstepping the limits of the inherited tradition. These cases clearly demonstrate that language is not independent of human will, that it functions as a tool of cultural interchange and that it can be molded and folded in accordance with its user's inclinations. Written language is divided into separate traditions of writing but on occasion these traditions may be shuffled and reshuffled as a pack of cards.

9. Registers and individual choice: an example

My main field of study is history of the Russian language. Let me give my last example from the history of this language. It is particularly resourceful for studying the interaction between various traditions of writing because medieval Rus' received its written language in conjunction with Christian catechism from Southern Slavs. As a consequence, there was from the start a considerable difference between written and spoken languages and extensive variation within the written language, which in the process of development gave rise to a variety of written traditions. Their interplay is manifested by a multitude of texts.

To illustrate, cited is a simple example from the history of Russian grammar. There were two forms of infinitive in Old Russian, one in

-ti and another in *-t'*. The last one was a newer form, the result of the apocope of the final vowel. In the spoken language the new form supplanted the old one quite early, say, in the fourteenth century. In the written language, however, the old form continued to be used for many centuries. Where there is variation there is also a possibility of choice. Different written traditions demonstrated a preference for one or the other form. In particular, the old form in *-ti* was used almost exclusively in religious literature (I might note in passing that practically all medieval Russian literature was religious).

However, there were occasional exceptions. One of them was a text called *The Life of Archpriest Avvakum* written by himself, from the second half of the seventeenth century. It is a curious narrative. It is at the same time a saint's life (with miracles, ascetic deeds, and other proper attributes) and the first Russian autobiography. Avvakum was one of the leaders of the Old Believers, a religious movement in many respects reminiscent of the Reformist dissent in various Western countries. They preached repentance, moral transformation and eradication of pernicious customs and habits. Avvakum strove to present himself as a model of the true believer, as a righteous man struggling with impious persecutors. He could not, however, declare himself to be a saint. He constructed the authority of his text in a very elaborate way. He narrated his life in a distinctly colloquial style (though intermingled with passages written in lofty bookish language); orality of the style served to demonstrate Avvakum's humility. One of the most prominent features of this imitation of orality is the pervasive use of the new form of the infinitive; the old form occurs mostly in bookish passages. In this respect Avvakum's autobiography differs strikingly from his other writings, devotional and theological, which preserve the traditional use of the old form of the infinitive. On the basis of Avvakum's strategy of using language, we can conclude that a medieval writer was not obliged to choose to use only a single tradition of writing, a writer could be the master of several traditions and use them to shape his text in accordance with his or her rhetorical tasks.

We may reach the same conclusion by analyzing the forms of the infinitive in chancellery texts. Usually only the new form (without a vowel) is used in them. However, there are minutes of judicial investigation in which the whole text is written exclusively with the new forms, with the exception of the conclusion. The conclusion, in which the tsar's final verdict is given, abounds in old forms. Evidently they are used with the special purpose of marking this part of the proceedings as particularly solemn and important. Here again we observe how language is manipulated by individuals, how it functions as a tool of human culture rather than a superimposed elemental force to which human culture is subordinated.

10. Conclusion

Let us in closing return to tradition. Language consists of elements belonging to various cultural traditions. Speech is generated not so much by an abstract mechanism, as by human understanding. Speakers and writers produce their texts as an amalgamated unity; its constituent elements point out to different (multiple) allegiances and identities of the individual. Language is immersed in history, and texts in the process of their appearance build up the future out of the inherited past.

References

[1]   Kurath, H. and McDavid R.I. (1961) *The Pronunciation of English in the Atlantic States. Based upon the Collections of the Linguistic Atlas of the Eastern United States,* Ann Arbor, Michigan. In the interpretation of these facts I follow Alan Timberlake, See Timberlake, A. (2002) 'Signficatio, Conventio, Imitatio et Inventio', *Russkii iazyk v nauchnom oveshchenni,* 4, in Russian.

[2]   Yates, F. (1984) *The Art of Memory,* London, Routledge.

[3]   Castells, M. (1996) *The Rise of the Network Society,* Cambridge, Massachusetts, Blackwell Publishers.

[4]   Collins, S. (1671) *The Present State of Russia, in a letter to a friend at London, written by a eminent person residing at the Tzars court at Moscow for the space of nine years,* London, Printed by J. Winter for D. Newman.

Tradition and Innovation in the Common Law

Michael Lobban

1. Introduction

In his *Commentaries on the Laws of England*, published between 1765 and 1769, Sir William Blackstone wrote of the common law,

> We inherit an old gothic castle, erected in the days of chivalry, but fitted up for a modern inhabitant. The moated ramparts, the embattled towers, and the trophied halls, are magnificent and venerable, but useless. The inferior apartments, now converted into rooms of convenience, are chearful and commodious, though their approaches are winding and difficult.

Blackstone's architectural simile was intended to show how the law had grown over a period of time, portraying it as a building in which we live. If there were some parts that no longer served a function, still they provided a sense of continuity. If there were inconveniences in living in an ancient structure, still it had been adapted to present purposes and could not be torn down. Blackstone's work was in many ways a defence of the common law, at a time when delays in procedure, expense in litigation and vexation from lawyers was a matter of much public debate. From the commentator, the problem did not lie with the old common law, but with careless changes: 'to say the truth' he said, 'almost all the perplexed questions, almost all the niceties, intricacies and delays which have sometimes disgraced the English, as well as other courts of justice, owe their original not to the common law itself, but to innovations that have been made in it by acts of parliament.'

Michael Lobban

Michael Lobban is Professor of Legal History at Queen Mary, University of London. He was educated at the University of Cambridge and has taught at Oxford and Durham, as well as in London. He is the author of *The Common Law and English Jurisprudence, 1760–1850* (Oxford, 1991), as well as of a number of articles on the history of English law. He has recently completed a short history of Anglo-American legal thought.

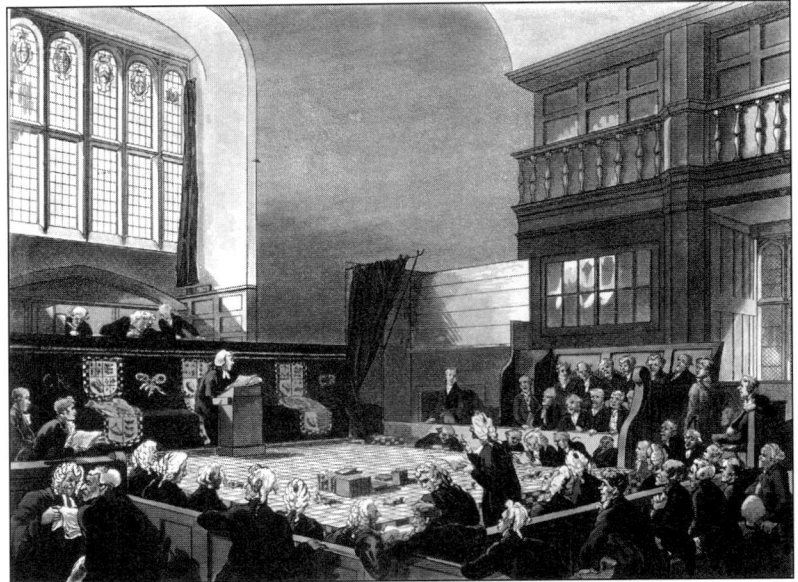

'Court of Exchequer'
By permission of The British Library.

In defending the age of the common law, and the wisdom of leaving it in the hands of those who knew and understood it, Blackstone was repeating an argument that had been made by jurists in the centuries preceding his. Common lawyers were conservative when it came to their law and they made great claims for its antiquity. In 1470, the lawyer Serjeant Catesby remarked that the common law had in fact been in existence since the creation of the world. A few years earlier, the Chief Justice Sir John Fortescue claimed that not only was English law the best there was, but that 'the realm has been continuously ruled by the same customs as it is now.' Yet even these lawyers did not see the whole law as static: it was not the detail of the law that remained unchanged, but only its underlying principles. By the time the first history of the common law was written in the mid-seventeenth century, by Sir Matthew Hale, the fiction of a static unchanging common law had been dropped. Now, the common law was compared with a body which grew over time. It was, he said, like Titius, who 'is the same man he was 40 years since, tho' the physicians tell us, that in a tract of seven years, the body has scarce any of the same material substance it had before.'

2. Custom and the common law

What was this common law which the jurists lauded? Sir John Davies, Attorney General for Ireland in the reign of James I, defined it as 'nothing else but the *Common Custome* of the Realm' which was 'recorded and registered no-where but in the memory of the people.' Davies said that customs developed in this way: 'When a reasonable act once done is found to be good and beneficial to the people, and agreeable to their nature and disposition, then they do use it and practice it again and again, and so by often iteration and multiplication of the act it becomes a *Custom*; and being continued without interruption time out of mind, it obtains the force of a *Law*.' His contemporary, Sir Edward Coke, proclaimed the common law to be the perfection of reason, albeit not the reason of any particular individual. For, 'if all the reason that is dispersed into so many several heads were united into one,' he said, 'yet he could not make such a law as the Law of England is, because by many succession of ages it hath been fined and refined by an infinite number of grave and learned men, and by long experience grown to such a perfection'. Hale agreed. Against Thomas Hobbes, who argued that law should be what the reason of the ruling sovereign specified, Hale retorted 'it is reason for me to prefer a Law by which a kingdom has been happily governed four or five hundred years, than to adventure the happiness and peace of a kingdom upon some new theory of my own, though I am better acquainted with the reasonableness of my own theory than with that law.' In these ideas, we see the germ of Edmund Burke's conception of the English constitution, articulated at the time of the French Revolution, as being a partnership between the living, the dead and those yet to be born.

As these men pointed out, the common law derives ultimately from custom, whose origins can only be searched for in the distant past: Many of the central institutions in our constitution evolved slowly in the past. We cannot give a single date for the creation of the superior courts of law or equity, for the institution of the jury, or the institution of parliament. Each grew over a period of time in answer to specific problems. The king's courts and the jury must be sought for prior to the beginning of the reign of Richard the Lionheart in 1189, the date used by lawyers to define the limit of legal memory. They are by definition immemorial; and (as the Blair government found when proposing to abolish the office of Lord Chancellor), they form a part of the national heritage that is hard to uproot. Of course, to call the common law a customary system is slightly misleading. Although its foundations are customary, the custom that makes up most of the common law is the custom of the courts as interpreters of the law. For Coke, Hale and Blackstone, knowledge of the law was to be found by an 'artificial reason', the reason of those trained and knowledgeable in law. As they saw it, lawyers who argued in court and who studied their profession would understand the reason of the principles of the law which were often opaque to the wider public. Those learned in law would be able to draw the principles out of the cases, and apply those principles to new situations. In taking this view, they did not say that all the common law was the creation of the lawyers: but that lawyers were the mediators and interpreters of custom.

3. Reforming the law

Over the centuries, this common law tradition has periodically encountered attempts to reform it anew. Coke, for instance, feared the ambitions of James I, who had plans to unite the laws of England and Scotland into a new code. Seventeenth century jurists feared that the writing down of the laws might lead to the importation of an alien Roman law tradition, with absolutist overtones. The most serious threat to the common law, however, came almost two hundred years later. The late eighteenth century was an era of the writing of new codes of law on the continent of Europe, as nations forged new identities and used rewriting of law as part of that process. Famous examples are the code for Prussia introduced by Frederick the Great, and the Code Napoleon, enacted after the turn of the nineteenth century in France.

In England, the great champion of the code was Jeremy Bentham – who has his own place in architectural history, for his plan to build a panopticon prison, which he finally gave up only in 1802. Some historians have seen in his prison a paradigm of Bentham's society. His prison was a circular building, with a central inspection area in the middle, and cells around the exterior. From the central lodge, the prison governor would exercise constant surveillance over all the prisoners, while not being observed by them. Similarly, Bentham's state would have a strong legislature passing criminal laws to control and shape people's behaviour in the name of utility. Whether or not this is a fair representation – and it has been challenged by recent work – it is beyond dispute that Bentham hated the common law, and that he wished to see it replaced by a new complete code, preferably written by him. In his view, the common law as developed in the courts was equivalent to the law a man gave his dog: he waited until the dog misbehaved and then beat him for it. So with the common law. No person knew whether his or her conduct was right or wrong until after a court decided; and of course the decision penalised someone. In his view, it would be far better to start afresh, creating a new system of law, where everyone would know in advance what was legal and what not and where the newly created law would be best tailored to the current needs of society.

Jeremy Bentham never managed to draft a complete code of laws. Nor was a code enacted, even in the area which seemed most fit for it, the criminal law – though efforts towards a code continue to this day. But for much of the nineteenth century, both in England and America, there were continued debates over whether the unwritten common law should be written into a new code. Those who opposed it looked over the English Channel, to the writings of the German jurist, Friedrich Carl von Savigny, a staunch opponent of codification and founder of an Historical School of jurisprudence. Savigny said that a nation's laws were like its language: they grew with the development of the people and expressed the national spirit – the *Volksgeist*. English lawyers were less romantic in their conception, but they shared the hostility to fixed codes of law. In their view, if one was to rely only on the words of a code, cases would inevitably arise which had never cropped up before and for which the code provided no clear answer or at least an unsatisfactory one. Common lawyers who had once championed the timelessness of their system now stressed its advantage as a growing law, and a law of principles. If the judge did not have a black-letter answer to the question before him, he would at least understand the principles and notions of the tradition of the common law, which would be adapted to the new case as it arose. Instead of the judge simply giving his own opinion, he would be the interpreter of the opinion of the community, as expressed in the principles of its laws. Secondly, as a corollary to this, they were concerned that to write a single code would fix the law at one point in time: so that future generations would not be ruled by a living law, but by a set of views which might be out of date.

4. Traditions guiding the legal community

In this view, we see the notion articulated that the tradition of the common law was a developing one. We find this articulated in the famous aphorism of Oliver Wendell Holmes, professor at Harvard Law School in the 1880s and justice of the US Supreme Court in the first three decades of the twentieth century. Holmes asserted that 'The life of the law has not been logic; it has been experience.' In making this point, Holmes argued that to understand the law, one needed to trace its history, to see the ways in which doctrines had developed and the reasons why they had developed. This meant that one could both see what was an important part of the law, the tradition to be kept and what was no longer of use, since its foundations had ceased to support the structure. Without history, Holmes later wrote, we cannot know the precise scope of the rules of law: but he found it revolting to have no better reason for a law than that it had been laid down in the distant past. Holmes therefore sought to look forward as well as back.

'For the rational study of the law,' he wrote, 'the man of the future is the man of statistics and the master of economics'.

5. Common law adjudication

Holmes identified a central problem: how should current judges facing modern problems take into account the inheritance of the past? How can past traditions meet present needs and what should be done if the voices of history tell a tale that is unsuitable for the present? The question can be answered by looking at the job of lawyers and judges. How, it may be asked, do they know what the law is? It is easily assumed that to find an answer, the lawyer should merely go to the library and find the rule in the relevant statute or the precedent case. But of course the very fact that a case goes to court – or at least to a higher court – is an indication that the law is uncertain, either with respect to what a particular rule means or even with respect to whether a rule exists at all. How do judges settle cases when there is such doubt? We would all agree that judges should not simply toss a coin to decide it, for they need to give reasoned arguments. We would also agree that they should not simply give moral or political arguments, in effect making a new rule by themselves that will bind in future cases. As judges, we expect them to act judicially and leave law-making to parliament. At the same time, judges cannot refuse to decide cases if there is no clear rule to guide them. They therefore need to look more deeply into the legal system than just locating rules. As the jurist Ronald Dworkin has pointed out, law is not just a collection of *rules*, for solving cases also involves looking to broader legal *principles*, which reflect the tradition and values of the legal community and through it the wider community. This can be seen from the celebrated New York case of *Riggs* v. *Palmer* in 1889, where a court had to decide whether an heir named in his grandfather's will could inherit under the will, even though he had murdered his grandfather to do so. On a literal construction of the relevant statute of wills of New York, he was entitled to inherit: but the court added that all laws, and so all wills, 'may be controlled in their operation and effect by the general, fundamental maxims of the common law.' One such maxim was that no man should profit by his own wrong: and so the grandson did not inherit. Legal principles, it may be suggested, concern larger notions of justice and fairness derived from the legal practices of the community.

This means that when judges make decisions in difficult or novel cases, although the decisions they make may be original, they are informed by legal tradition. As Dworkin has written,

> Institutional history acts not as a constraint on the political judgment of judges but as an ingredient of that judgment, because institutional history is part of the background that any plausible judgment about the right of an individual must accommodate. Political rights are creatures of both history and morality: what an individual is entitled to have, in civil society, depends upon both the practice and the justice of its political institutions.

In novel cases, the judge will nevertheless have to make a *new* decision, not merely apply a simple answer from the past. In doing so, Dworkin has argued, the judge must identify the legal rules and principles that are relevant and then give them the best interpretation for their community. Judges are, he says, in some senses in the position of a person taking part in writing a 'chain novel', where different chapters are written one after another by different authors. The writer of each chapter will be constrained by having to make his story fit with what has been set before and will advance the story by making the best constructive interpretation of the material available. In a similar manner, for Dworkin, any interpretation of the law must fit with the historical legal record. However, the interpretation the judge gives is not the one that best explains the original reason for the rule, but which speaks best for the community now.

This may also entail recognising the need to close the chapter on rules that have outlived their time. This can be seen from the well-known case of *R* v. *R* 1992 1 AC 599, where the House of Lords ruled that a man could be convicted of the rape of his wife. In so deciding, the highest court in the land abolished the common law rule which stated that upon her marriage, a wife irrevocably consented to her husband's exercise of his marital rights. This rule had existed for several hundreds of years and was to be found in the classic legal treatises on crime dating from Sir Matthew Hale's seventeenth century *Pleas of the Crown*. In so doing, the court effectively did what Holmes said should be done: it looked at the nature and history of a doctrine and said that its reason no longer applied. In his ruling in the case, Lord Lane CJ said, 'where the common law rule no longer even remotely represents what is the true position of a wife in present day society, the duty of the court is to take steps to alter the rule if it can legitimately do so... this is not the creation of a new offence, it is the removal of a common law fiction which has become anachronistic and offensive.' The case is important for showing that the courts will not feel bound by tradition to decisions they feel radically out of step with present needs. But *R* v. *R* is important for another reason: the court had never abolished a common law doctrine before. That was always seen to be the task of parliament. This looks at one glance as a radical innovation: but if we look back at the understanding of the nature of the common law as it has developed over time, we may argue that perhaps it was a manifestation of the Burkean tradition and not its negation.

6. Architecture and law

Tradition and innovation have always gone together in the history of the common law, a system which has been based on developing the law incrementally to reflect the needs and mores of the society it serves. In the same way, lawyers have sought to marry tradition and innovation in their working environment. The judges have themselves long inhabited Gothic buildings – if not Blackstone's castle – but sought on occasion to fit them to new conditions, while still remaining faithful to the past. When royal courts of justice were first established in the later twelfth century, Westminster Hall had already been built, and it would remain – physically and psychologically – at the heart of English law. Until the mid-eighteenth century, four courts sat simultaneously in this Hall, without being partitioned off from each other. In this building, the King's judges had to contend with competing noise from booksellers, spectators, and even dogs. Such informality could not last. Just as Blackstone's *Commentaries* sought to put the law into a new modern frame, so in his age a new set of buildings was put up abutting Westminster Hall. Extended by Sir John Soane in 1822–4, they came to hide the ancient Hall from view, though a sentiment for the Gothic led to adjustments being made to the building, to pay homage to it. These buildings survived the fire which destroyed parliament in 1834, though they remained unloved, both by the legal profession which found them cramped and inconvenient and by Barry, who wished to pull them down. But while the Court of Chancery moved to Lincoln's Inn in the nineteenth century, the new courts at Westminster remained in use until the Royal Courts of Justice were finally built and opened in 1882, after decades of wrangling. This neo-Gothic building not only paid homage to the age of the law, but more importantly brought the judges to the site of the Inns of Court, where lawyers had lived and worked since the fourteenth century.

Like its architecture, the common law has never been static, but has grown both as new cases and new problems arose in society which needed resolution in court, and as an increasing volume of legislation has contributed to shape our legal polity. The development of law has continued in recent years with the addition of new rules and principles, particularly after the accession of the United Kingdom to the European Union. The Human Rights Act of 1998, which incorporates the European Convention on Human Rights into UK law, will unquestionably have a major impact. However, each rule must be digested into the system, and must be interpreted and applied by judges steeped in the mentality of the common law mind. Titius continues to grow.

TRADITION & DIVERSITY

Tradition and Diversity in Food and Gastronomy

Lynne Chatterton

Lynne Chatterton

Lynne Chatterton was born in the South Australian Riverland – a land of oranges, vines and vegetables. She has travelled and worked extensively in many developing countries to improve the farming on small farms. She now lives in Umbria among forests and olive trees. She has grown food commercially and in her own garden, written about food, worked with governments to improve food and cooked food for many years.

1. Introduction

Gastronomy is the art of choosing, cooking and eating good food. I wish to tackle this subject from the point of view of the new tradition surrounding food that has been created in our lifetime. This new tradition has almost entirely driven out the old traditions that we associated with food for centuries.

2. Our food today

It began when working men and women exchanged payment in kind for cash wages. As cities grew and more people lived in urban centres without access to land, a dependence on food that came not from the farm or garden but from the shop and warehouse intensified. International trade in food expanded from imports of spices and dried herbs to chilled and tinned produce and this accustomed consumers to processed food. Nonetheless, until two or three generations ago most of the food that we ate was recognizably natural produce and cooked in the home. Most of our traditional food today comes precooked and packaged from the supermarket, the restaurant, the take-away and the delicatessen on the corner. It is the food our children will recall with nostalgia in their old age.

What has this done to our old traditions in food?

(a) For a start we are rapidly losing the traditional close link between food and the land in or on which it is grown.

(b) An insidious adulteration of our taste buds has taken place. The flavour of fresh produce is to most only a faint memory.

(c) The microwave and freezer have supplanted the wood stove and the kitchen range.

(d) We no longer choose our food by its original colour, freshness, shape or taste. Today the desirability is assessed by the image on the packet or jar, by the celebrity chef who has created a pretty recipe on television, in a glossy book, magazine or a newspaper or by the account of what some food writer has eaten with a friend in an expensive restaurant.

Foccacia.

3. Labels

The hyperbole on the labels of the food we buy is able to convince us that what we buy is the real thing because sadly many people do not even know there is a difference.

The image also suggests to us that by buying these packets, jars and tins we will be engaging in the comforts of traditional food as it used to be. These are all comforting, warm, sociable characteristics.

4. Old traditional food

(a) Was prepared and cooked by women and men in the home.

(b) The staples for its dishes came with little intervention between the land and the table.

(c) Its associated ingredients were available according to natural rhythms – they were seasonal and determined by the local climate.

(d) Each dish had a distinctive taste.

(e) Part of the enjoyment of food was that it was taken in company.

Hardly any of these attributes can be found in our food today.

5. Ethnic food and tradition

Some of us try to satisfy our desire for old traditional food by buying ethnic food. We read romantic accounts of dishes that have for

Detail of "September",
from series of plates showing the Labours of the
Hours, after a mediaeval image.

Detail of "July",
from series of plates showing the Labours of the
Hours, after a mediaeval image.

centuries been the traditional food of Asia, Arabia, the Mediterranean basin – Greece, Turkey, Italy and France – it seems to promise what we crave.

We once despised the olive oil, the garlic, and the curry spices that give it flavour – now we seek them avidly.

We want to be part of a tradition where food comes from real kitchens, made by women, fresh from daily markets, chattering away all day as they chop and pound and stir robust, aromatic traditional food, that is then served and eaten at large, cheerful gatherings around well laden tables.

Unfortunately, most of us rely on restaurants, supermarkets and take-aways to slake our desire for this food and so pale and often distorted imitations of the original are now widely eaten here and in Australia, America and New Zealand.

Does traditional ethnic food really live up to the image we have of it? In some ways it does, in others it does not.

For the big feast it is indeed much as we imagine.

The day to day reality is different. Peasant woman don't have much time to cook and they have a very limited range of ingredients and utensils with which to cook. They must tend the children, hoe in the fields, walk for water and for the food they must buy, harvest and conserve the food they grow, gather firewood, keep their habitation as clean as possible, wash the clothes, and milk the sheep or goats. They rely on dishes left to cook slowly all day and food that can be prepared rapidly and simply. It is in fact convenience food, but of a nature very different to ours. It has little variety but it is healthy food and families and friends eat it together several times every day.

For example, before 1960 the traditional diet of rural Italians was frugal. Men and women tended to be short in stature and often appeared old before their time. Today Italians in general are taller, robust, straight limbed and long lived. The variety in their diet is remarkably little changed but in a prosperous Italy they eat more of it and flourish.

Other Italian traditions still prevail. Italians do not like novelty in food. Restaurants who try it are left without clients. The most popular restaurants cook the food Italians prepare and eat in their kitchens at home. Company is obligatory in Italy – especially at the table.

Within ethnic cultures, the actual preparation of food, the relevance of its seasonality, its serving and its eating have as much importance in the stability and strength of its traditions as do the ingredients. Food and its place in life is experience and is passed on as such. No one learns to cook from a book.

By the time girls are teenagers, the dishes they cook, the bread they make are automatic operations that they perform each day. The marketing, growing, gathering, the management of seasonal flushes and winter scarcities, the pots and pans and table manners are part of their lives and they pass it all on in their turn.

Men know about food too. When we were working with young male agricultural technicians in the Middle East and North Africa the easiest way to break down defenses and prejudices was to ask how to cook the food we were eating at lunch on the first working day. They would become enthusiastic and animated as they described the minutiae of the process.

6. Our tradition and how it has changed

Our traditional convenience food exists within a very different culture. We eat on the run, we eat out, we don't often eat together, if we learn to cook at all it is from a book. But most notable of all, the prepared food that we buy for the convenience that we seek so assiduously is no longer the food it once was. How has this come about? Consider the following components of a convenient healthy breakfast:

Orange juice used to be squeezed from the fruit as we needed it. When the simple orange squeezer was invented it was a great leap forward. It took the elbow out of the job. Then someone thought up a way to squeeze the fruit on a production line, put it in plastic packs and sell it in shops. Preservative was added to extend its shelf life.

Cheap apple juice was used to break down the more expensive orange juice, and later Brazilian orange concentrate made the drink even cheaper. By this time sugar was needed to give the liquid some taste. This became 'orange fruit drink'. It sold at the same price as orange fruit juice. Some consumers read the small print on the labels and kicked up a fuss. So the processors recreated 'pure orange juice' sold it as a quality product and put the price up. Most consumers stuck to the 'orange fruit drink' because it was cheap and the taste had become familiar.

This chain of events put many traditional orange growers out of production – their prices went down when substitutes diminished the demand for their fruit and when the quality 'natural orange juice' came in, they were paid no part of the processors' enhanced profits.

Now let's take one of the oldest traditional foods – yoghurt. Thirty years ago the only yoghurt most of us ever ate was when we visited India or the Middle East or Greece. It was made from sheep's milk, was pleasantly acidic and made us feel good. Very healthy. Then the production line began. Cow's milk was used because it was cheap and readily available. The first pots were a little thin and sour so fruit was added. It tasted like discarded jam, but probably wasn't – just cheap

The Pleasure of Eating Together.

fruit pulp with preservative added together with a bit of dextrose to sweeten and a bit of artificial flavouring to boot.

Then milk was targeted as a contributor to blocked arteries and obesity so whole milk was replaced by de-fatted milk. Lately a thickening agent has been added to provide a semblance of substance; artificial flavours swamp any remaining natural flavour. Consumers feel virtuous and healthy when they eat yoghurt. They believe that if they eat enough of it they will lose weight and they will – it has very little nourishment left in it. They will lose weight but they won't be healthy. There are a few small producers who do their best to provide a natural yoghurt but this is seldom seen among displays of commercial product. Most consumers don't like natural yoghurt – it is too sour.

As for muesli, I doubt many people remember when Dr Gayelord Hauser introduced muesli to bemused nutritionists in the 1950s. It was a direct challenge to the then traditional breakfast cereal, cornflakes. Muesli had no added sugar, no salt, and no fat. It was simply an uncooked mixture of grains, dried fruit and nuts. In the USA there were even attempts to make it illegal.

The enticement of its healthy attributes led to it becoming popular so the processors decided to create their own version. Their muesli contains sugar, fat, cornflakes, coconut shreds, and salt. Coconut contains one of the highest of the saturated oils, and salt, sugar, fat, and processed cornflakes were the very ingredients that muesli rejected for reasons of health. Today processed muesli is ubiquitous and available toasted and made crackly with even more sugar. Few people even know what Hauser muesli tastes like. Commercial muesli is big business; no one would dare to try to make its promotion illegal.

In each of these cases there has been a series of interventions between the food grown in the earth and the food we eat. We no longer make these foods at home. We conveniently buy them in the supermarket. In each intervention the natural taste of the food is changed either because the natural sugars are lost in the lead time from farm to table because something is added to the original food or

The Pleasure of Cooking.

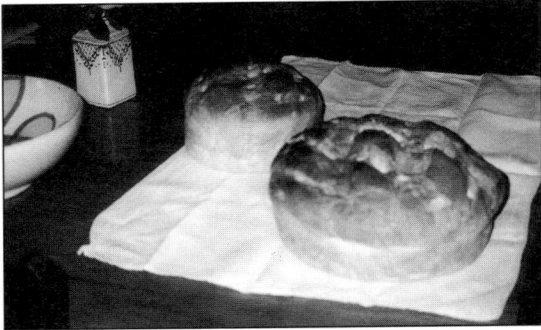

Homemade Bread – So Little Work.

Herbs fresh from the garden.

because it is chemically changed through processing. The traditional values of taste and nourishment have been traded for today's tradition of convenience.

7. Political intervention

Other interventions that shape our food today originate in a political desire to 'organise' agriculture, to facilitate international trade, to improve standards of hygiene. In the process they develop a life of their own, become amorphous, all-pervading and very powerful.

Farmers who work small holdings, consumers and village shopkeepers simply do not have the political clout to resist the decisions of these powerful interests.

Those involved in hands-on food farming are a minority.

Most people have little or no idea of the operations on the farm.

The very language of farming is becoming arcane.

Agriculture is assuming the status of a mystique.

Most people are unaware of the relationship between the dictates of officialdom and the effect these have on farmers and their own food.

8. Subsidies

For instance:

Subsidies decided and administered by officials are making a huge difference to the food available to us.

In the UK the largesse of the Common Agricultural Policy has benefited the big farmers – mainly cereal farmers and livestock producers i.e. those who went with the slogans of the 70s – 'get big or get out' and 'farming is not a way of life but a business'. Generally, subsidies are targeted to the barely edible. Rarely is an incremental subsidy paid for higher quality.

Many farmers have been forced by regulations, often tied to subsidies, into environmentally costly industrial farming. Hands-on farmers who farm in harness with nature and take quality and nutritive value into account cannot compete and they are forced out of business.

In Italy, on the other hand, CAP subsidies have enabled farm families on mixed farms to not only survive but to do so comfortably. In the region of Umbria the majority of the farms are of this type and in a complex manner the CAP subsidies support not only the farm families but also the local community. Of course there are 'cash crops' of sunflowers and tobacco that no one really needs and lashings of olive trees and vines for a market that will collapse when they all come into production, but there is also good supplies of fresh and rapidly available food.

In Australia where there are no subsidies, farmers on big properties must compete on world markets with low-cost farming and biting the bullet of drought. Fruit and vegetable growers and dairy farmers respond to local markets and have to deliver a quality product to survive.

9. Experts and expertise

Experts who make policy decisions that affect our food often know little about hands-on farming or about food. Hands-on farmers frequently writhe in pained amusement at the pontifications of the movers and shakers in today's food industry. Economists in particular.

A book recently appeared written by a distinguished microbiologist. At the end of his wise advice on food hygiene was a list of recipes, which he put forward as desirable for a healthy diet. They were terrible – full of tins of this and that, high in sugar and fat and worst of all, tasteless.

10. Hygiene – does it help?

Governments intervene in the name of hygiene in the way food is grown and the processes that bring it to us. Much of this is justified because the lead time from farm to kitchen has increased enormously since supermarkets became the source of today's traditional food.

We know only too well the risk of spoilage and disease due to the passage of food on and off planes and ships from foreign countries, the movement of food from farm to central depot for packaging and then out to sales points, not to mention the handling that takes place

The fruits of autumn.

Rowan James, Grocers Shop, 2005.
Reproduced by permission of The Prince's
Drawing School.

as produce is cut and portioned, wrapped and packaged. Plastic wrap that has taken over from brown paper and tissue is, in my opinion, not only a health hazard but often a physical danger.

Many regulations supposedly promulgated for purposes of hygiene are designed to keep out competitive imports or to make standardised marketing easier.

The growing and sale of local produce are often impossible due to costly hygiene requirements devised to deal with supermarket fallibility. Locally gown and sold produce does not present the health risk that processed, conveyor belt products do. If less rigorous standards were allowed for produce grown and sold locally this would improve our traditional food.

11. Globalisation

Globalisation has swept away many old traditions in food and many traditional growers of food. In some ways it has enlarged our diets. It is why migrants can recreate in the UK more or less the traditional peasant food they are used to and why we find semblances of it in our food outlets.

But globalisation goes hand in hand with global standards for food products. These are a boon for global corporations because they support production line techniques. Factories can insist that fruit and vegetables are a uniform size and type. Everything else is refused. Farmers are forced to grow only varieties that simplify the cannery throughput never mind the flavour. I have seen tonnes of peaches, tomatoes, oranges thrown away when a canning factory becomes the major outlet for farm produce.

12. GM crops

Genetically modified seed is another destroyer of old traditional food but it will be an important determinator of new traditions in food. It saves on sprays and standardises crops but we will lose even more of the eccentricity of variety which is fundamental to good food.

The late summer harvest.

13. Taste buds

In the recent tantrum over where the new European Food Standards Agency should be located – Helsinki or Parma – ('Do the Finns know what taste is?' asked a well known leader) it was asserted that the 'FSA is not about taste – it's about quality'. And that is the rub. Quality of food is very much related to taste. Without the distinction of flavour it becomes not food with a recognisable identity, but fodder.

14. Supermarkets

Supermarkets are the greatest interventionists of all between natural, simple food and our tables. Supermarkets are dear to our hearts.

They are a social outing, a stimulus and the hub of today's traditional food.

But they have wielded the biggest axe in the battle between old traditions in food and the new tradition we now have. It is in their interests that we buy processed food because this is where they make their profits. The wind and water that puff out most convenience foods today are the cheapest ingredients of all.

We barely realise that we pay for production lines, additives, packaging, transport and distribution, advertising, image creation, administration, management, elaborate buildings, refrigeration, parking lots, regulators, inspections, customs, security services and we pay the supermarket shareholder profit. No wonder the prices paid to hands-on farmers are low – his/her product is perishable and there is no bargaining strength there.

15. What to do?

The question we have to ask ourselves is: does it matter that our current traditional food has been created for us by officials, questionable experts, supermarkets and corporations?

We are not going to give up all that convenience, even when it is demonstrated unequivocally that the convenience is not for us. No matter how much we deplore it, this is now our tradition. Even food

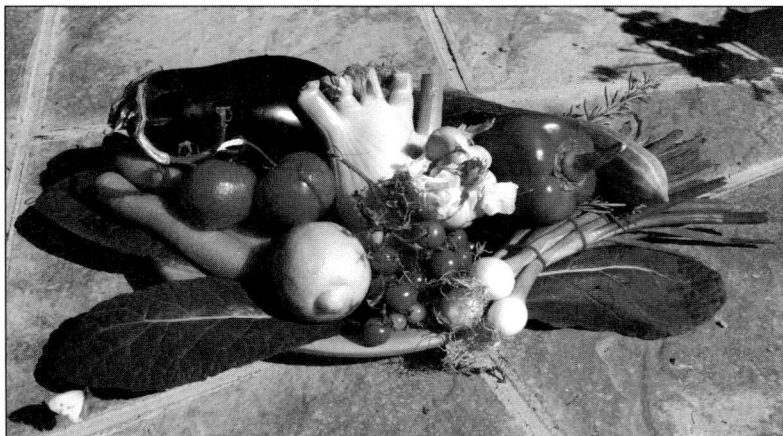

writers who clamour most for local produce, fresh ingredients and home cooked food list convenience foods in their recipes.

16. Cultural change?

Many of us have this nostalgic yearning for the pleasure and simple nourishment that used to be synonymous with food.

Is it possible to integrate a more satisfying food culture into our increasingly dysfunctional tradition?

Cooking and preparation of food would certainly have to be restored as a worthwhile task – not as a demeaning, time wasting operation. We truly, deeply believe that time spent in preparation in our own kitchens is time wasted – yet the time we waste in overcrowded vast supermarkets gathering together, queuing to pay for, and then transporting and unpacking so-called convenience foods is far greater. Traditional food of the past was convenience food because it was simple and nourishing – we have forgotten that in our craving for endless variety.

We are distanced from the simplicities of traditional food by a culture that nourishes celebrity chefs with their elaborate kitchen

The fruits of autumn.

utensils and recherché ingredients. These only deepen our dependence on the supermarket because the reality is that, at the end of a long day at work, it is too hard to pore over a recipe book – let alone to find the desirable ingredients – so much easier to pick up a frozen pack promising ready to eat versions of the delight.

We would have to re-establish the practice of eating together as a pleasure, not only because eating in company is part of the pleasure we miss, but also to provide some satisfaction to the one or several who do the cooking. If we do re-instate this tradition we will have to be content with simple food that stretches easily and that does not make a sacrifice of the cook. Monotonous and reliable peasant dishes? Or more supermarket goods in the freezer?

17. Conclusion

The good traditions associated with food – nourishment, links with the land, kinship and pleasure are part of any culture worth its name. Peasant societies have kept them because they have, historically, had little choice. Today they face threats of declining yields, loss of pasture, conflicts over water, invasive and inappropriate economic policies, wars and forced migrations and these may destroy what they have.

We have had too much choice and we have been seduced by the glitter of false convenience and image. We have been dilettante and lost control of our food. Can we reinstate the old traditional values we sigh for, or must we continue to suffer the new?

Tradition in the Architecture of Islam

Khaled Azzam

Khaled Azzam

Dr Khaled Azzam is the Director of The Prince's School of Traditional Arts (formerly known as the Visual Islamic and Traditional Arts, or VITA, programme) at the Prince's Foundation. Dr Azzam has practised as an architect in Egypt, Saudi Arabia, Jordan and the Gulf region and has been designing according to traditional Islamic design principles and building techniques.

1. Introduction

I come from a background that many readers may not be familiar with and this, in a way, forms the basis of the two main points I would like to discuss now: first, that one of the blessings of the modern so-called 'multi-cultural' world is that we can see similarities and differences between cultures and traditions; and second, that what we believe and what we teach at The Prince's School of Traditional Arts is that the concept of 'tradition' is both universal and timeless.

There are many things that different cultures with their different 'traditions' can learn from each other in today's world, and it is imperative, in the increasingly complex environment in which we live, that we seek to define clearly the meaning of this term. At The Prince's School of Traditional Arts we have been discussing, explaining, defining and clarifying 'Tradition' ever since we were founded over twenty years ago. During this time, we have come across several layers of meaning, which I would like to share.

2. What is tradition?

Tradition can be explained as the customs and manners of a particular society which are handed down from one generation to the next, mainly through what we know as an 'oral tradition.' It can also be understood as ancestral memories or myths; and these memories transcend the mere customs and mannerisms of our forefathers. These memories relate to where we come from as well as having an impact on where we are going. Ultimately, these memories and oral teachings have their

Evelyn Chiao: The Omayyad Mosque Courtyard in Old Damascus, 2006. Reproduced by permission of the artist.

source in Divine Revelation and should be transmitted with reverence, care and responsibility. Each generation may interpret them afresh as a means of guiding us on the 'straight path' into the future – but always referring back to the wisdom of our ancestors who in turn received their guidance from Above. Tradition is therefore a timeless memory, a fountain of pure running water to which one may constantly return in order to seek refreshment to continue life's journey.

Furthermore, tradition can be expressed as the 'right way of living'. This right way is always of its moment and of its age. Thus it is always contemporary – a state which is much more relevant than simply being modern. The Islamic tradition, which I come from and which I will concentrate on today, is based on Divine Revelation (the Qur'an was revealed by the angel Gabriel to the Prophet Muhammad) and therefore, in its origin and principle, transcends time. Since it is a principle, which provides guidelines, its application is not restrained

Evelyn Chiao: Street houses II, Hama, Syria 2006. Reproduced by permission of the artist.

by physical location or linear time: it is everywhere and always relevant. This is most obvious in the realm of Islamic architecture, which has thrived for centuries over a vast area and was – and is still – always of its time, answering the physical, social and cultural identity of the location.

The religion of Islam permeates into every aspect of man's life, leaving nothing untouched by the sacred. This, by extension, means that there is no differentiation between the sacred and the profane in the everyday life of the Muslim. There is simply a hierarchy of being, which had its roots in Divine Unity and which manifests itself at every level of existence. This sense of unity is most evident in the arts of the Islamic world; however, there is an important paradox that should be pointed out first: the Qur'an, the holy book of Islam, does not set a specific model for the form of Islamic art. There is no principle of composition described in the Qur'an which can form the framework of an artistic expression. Also, Islamic art cannot draw its inspiration from the divine law, the *Sharia*, which simply regulates the daily life of the Muslim community by setting limits and guidelines. Furthermore, one cannot attribute this expression of unity to religious feeling since, however intense the emotion may be, it is not enough to inspire the immense range and depth of this art. The root of this unity transcends the realm of emotion which is always necessarily subjective, vague and fluctuating: rather, it is a much deeper intellectual vision that is the basis of Islamic art; and here we must understand the term 'intellect' in its original sense.

The 'intellect' in Islamic philosophy (as well as in medieval Christian thought) is the faculty in man that gives intuitive knowledge of the absolute and timeless realities. Intellect or *'aql* in Arabic, is the capacity to perceive the concept of divine unity. It is thus on a much higher plane than reason. Islamic tradition teaches that man's fundamental quality is being endowed with an intellect capable of metaphysical knowledge and hence capable of creating an art expressive of an absolute reality. This faculty of the intellect is not only expressed in the gift of speech but also through artistic creation, through the careful

Evelyn Chiao: Street houses I, Hama, Syria 2006.
Reproduced by permission of the artist.

Adam Williamson:
Bismillah calligraphic stone carving, 2006.
Reproduced by permission of the artist.

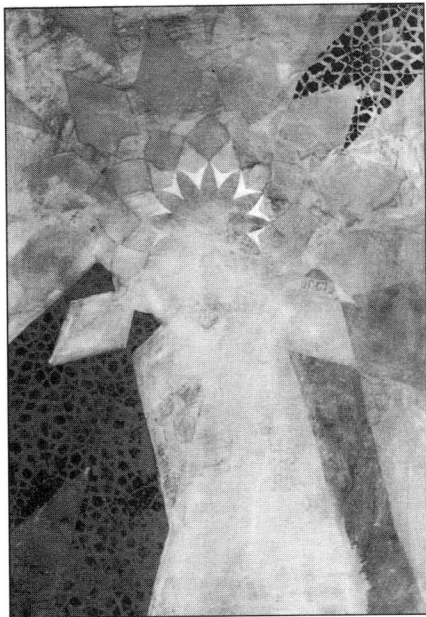

Lateefa Williamson: Geometric painting II, 2005. Reproduced by permission of the artist.

use of traditional forms with their inherent symbolic language. It is this vertical access, the direct link via the intellect with the higher levels of reality, which gives the process of work and craftsmanship, and the resulting artwork itself, its sacred dimension. It is from this wisdom that Islamic art derives its awe-inspiring beauty.

Art and architecture have always held a central role in the civilisation of Islam: a role that manifests the wide range of values that make up this civilisation. Although the art of calligraphy is considered to be the highest form of visual art since it expresses the Divine word, it is the art of architecture that encompasses the full range of disciplines and crafts, commonly identified with the Islamic world. These include masonry, carpentry and woodworking skills, ceramic tile-work and stained glass. Architecture is the setting for the different disciplines of the arts and crafts of Islam and it is evident that these arts and crafts do not exist for their own sake but exist to embellish and uplift our everyday life. Traditional architecture emerges from a particular community and environment and should be seen as an architecture of place and not an architecture of time – in that the solutions that have emerged in different regions are timeless, and can still be used (and often are) today. This process can be seen as traditional; it is in

Lateefa Williamson: Geometric painting I, 2005. Reproduced by permission of the artist.

Lateefa Williamson: Geometric painting III, 2006. Reproduced by permission of the artist.

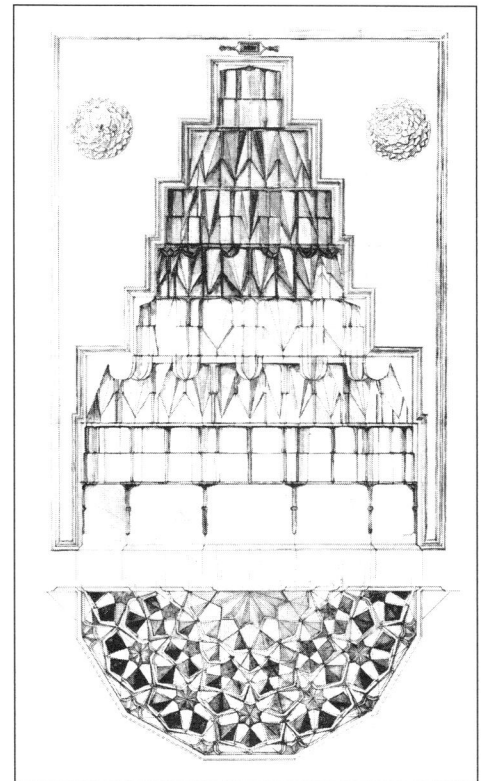

the nature of tradition to adapt and stay alive and constantly provide contemporary expressions of the timeless principles I referred to earlier. I have learnt a great deal from Hassan Fathy, a very wise Egyptian architect who inspired a whole generation of Arab architects. He once said that the basis of tradition in architecture is when two craftsmen on site find the solution to a particular problem and then teach it to another craftsman – that is the establishment of a tradition. It is as simple as that.

3. Harmony between architecture and the environment

Humankind's nature, the perennial wisdom tells us, is composed of body, soul and spirit, and thus any activity he undertakes necessarily contains an aspect of the realm of the spirit. The term 'ritual', the dictionary says, is specifically used to describe the performance of religious rites or acts; but today we often apply it to everyday apparently secular activities. The use of this word gives the activity great importance, an almost sacred dimension; and this, it has to be

Michael Gough: Painted door, 2000–2002.
Reproduced by permission of PSTA.

said, is not far from the truth because in essence all of humankind's activities are linked to Heaven in a greater or lesser degree. Traditional Islam (as with other sacred traditions, this is not exclusive to Islam by any means) sees the world as a reflection of Heaven. Everything that exists in this world – even the realms of ideas and imagination – is a reflection of a divine archetype. In this sense, a ritual signifies the re-enactment on earth of a divine archetype, an outward sign of an inner grace. The primordial nature (*fitrah* in Arabic) of the Islamic revelation means that emphasis is laid upon the peace and harmony that existed between humankind, God and nature before the Fall. This harmony between man and nature and vertical link with God is reflected in traditional Islamic architecture and city planning where the master-builders always sought the full integration of the built environment with its natural surroundings. The true Muslim sees himself as the custodian of nature (caliph or *khalifa* in Arabic means vice-regent; man is God's vice-regent on earth) and if he leaves an imprint on this physical space then it should be done with humility and with no sense of defiance to the natural order of being. Man in Islam is not the measure of all things but rather, the Muslim architect acknowledges by his Islam his submission to the divine will that God is the Supreme Architect. Thus the relationship between the architect and his surrounding space is one that is based on reverence and not arrogance – and there is no doubt that traditional Islamic architecture fully reflects this consciousness of the architect. There is never any attitude of conflict, defiance or conquest with the surrounding environment. This is seen in the harmony that exists between the traditional methods of construction and the use of natural materials – as expressed in the curves of domes, the fluid forms of vaults, the crenallations of the skyline, the recesses and protrusions of the walls, and the different craft activities and processes which all take place on site. This allows the buildings to interact gracefully with their surrounding space. Even the internal space of most buildings in the Arab world, the courtyard – which is metaphorically the heart of the building, is open to the sky, symbolising the aspiration of the heart towards heaven.

Haifa Khawaja: Blue tiles (bottom of a fountain), 2000–2002. Reproduced by permission of PSTA.

This sense of responsibility is evident if we observe some of the towns and cities that were built throughout the Islamic world. Some of these cities, such as Fez in Morocco and Isphahan in today's Iran, represent a height of urban life and sophistication unknown to mankind before our modern times. There is a recurring quality in these urban environments: it is the balance they maintain between the sophisticated urban lifestyle and the laws and rhythms of the natural order. Large cities, such as the two mentioned above, managed to exist and flourish without causing ecological disasters that we often associate with urban life today. The *medina* or the Islamic city is thus often described as a living organism, constantly alive and adapting according to the changing needs of its community. Yet contrary to first impressions, it is not a chaotic environment but one that is structured very clearly on the close integration of the everyday needs of the individual: worship, work, leisure, commerce and a sense of identity in a community. Islam does not divide the life of its community into sacred and profane domains – the sacred, as I have already pointed out, permeates through every aspect of the urban environment. Indeed, it is

Jamie Clark: Circular stained glass, 2003–2005. Reproduced by permission of PSTA.

Katya Nosyreva: Square ceramic tiles
(pale cream with red & black stars), 2003–2005.
Reproduced by permission of PSTA.

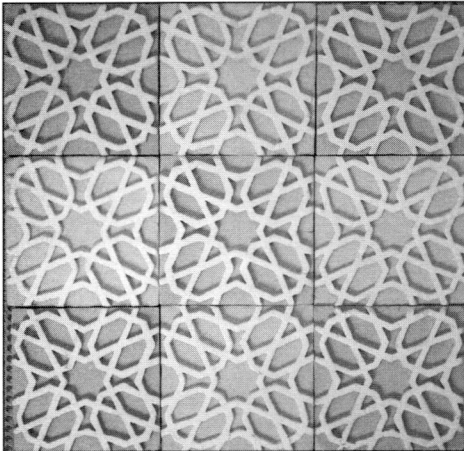

David Barnes: Square geometry tiles
(no glaze colours added), 2003–2005.
Reproduced by permission of PSTA.

a prime example of the relationship between the multiplicity of forms and the unity of principle. The architecture of Islam is thus more than just an aesthetic or spatial experience: it represents a symbolic vision of a higher reality.

4. Elements of Islamic architecture

If architecture is the art of ordering space, then sacred architecture extends the sense of order from physical space to an expression of a metaphysical order. The Islamic tradition teaches that without submission ('submission' or 'surrender' is one of the root meanings of the word *Islam*) there can be no true understanding, and without discipline there can be no flowering of the spirit that, in turn, leads to knowledge of the essential. This is most evident in the relationship between the fundamental aspects of Islamic art – namely, geometry, biomorphic form or arabesque, and calligraphy. Geometry is an objective manifestation of the principles of creation and forms the underlying framework for the visual expression of the path, which leads from unity to multiplicity and back to unity again. The arabesque or biomorphic forms, which symbolise virgin nature, would be unbalanced without the structure of the underlying geometry. Furthermore, both these art forms are the setting for calligraphy, the visual manifestation of the word of God as revealed in the Qur'an. The decoration of Islamic architecture with calligraphy, geometric patterns and arabesque interlacement should not be perceived simply as surface decoration: rather, it is a fundamental element in the overall composition of the architecture as well as being a manifestation of a higher order of being. It is cosmetic in the true sense of the word – to make 'cosmic-like'. The architect is inspired by the multiplicity of forms, patterns and rhythms he sees around him in nature and distils them to their fundamental essence: the undulating rhythms of the 'arabesque' are not recognisable plants observed in nature but are symbolic representations of nature's essential being. Thus the architect/artist/craftsman's work never stands separately from God's creation but is always a part of it.

This visual expression of the order of being is best represented through the discipline of geometry. Geometry is often mistaken for an artistic style, which it is not: it is the crystalline analysis of the working order of nature. The geometry is both quantitative and qualitative; its quantitative dimension regulates the form and construction of architecture while its qualitative nature sets the proportions of architectural form and represents an expression of the order of the universe, which regulates the cycle of manifestation. The proportions of sacred geometry derive from the division of a circle, the symbol of unity of being. Not only are the fundamental shapes of geometry related to heaven and earth respectively but the instruments that are used to draw them – that is the compasses and the set-square – have the same significance, the former representing heaven and the latter representing earth. The craftsman, when using these traditional tools, is participating in an age-old ritual of symbolically linking heaven and earth. The idea of the integration of the arts and the crafts with the principles of both beauty and function is not merely a philosophical

Ramiz Sabbagh: Hexagonal blue tile panel, 1999–2001. Reproduced by permission of PSTA.

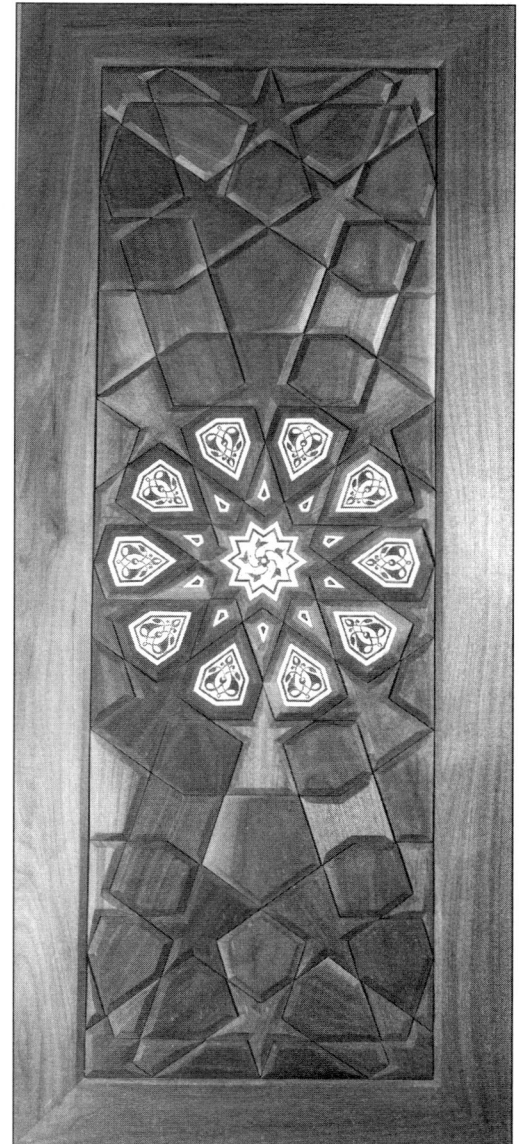

Ramiz Sabbagh: Wood door, 1999–2001. Reproduced by permission of PSTA.

Tarek El-Bouri:
Architectural drawing of arch, 1987–1989.
Reproduced by permission of PSTA.

one: it is a fact that has always existed in the architecture, city planning and communal life of the Muslim world.

Our examples of traditional Islamic art today are mainly drawn from ancient works often exhibited in museums. These works are not in their original context, nor do they perform their true function. Islamic art was never made simply for exhibition but to fulfil a certain function and convey a particular message within a given context. There was never any distinction between the fine and applied arts in the traditional Islamic world: to a greater or lesser degree all the arts of the Islamic world conveyed the highest principles and values. At the same time they remain central elements in the everyday life of the Muslim. However, although it seems that traditional Islamic art has – like traditional art the world over – been relegated to museums, it does in fact remain a living art still practised by craftsmen throughout the Islamic world, in spite of overwhelming obstacles. The work of contemporary craftsmen, which may be seen as a continuation of the same spirit of the ancient works exhibited in the museums, represents more than just an education for our eyes, hands and mind: it has an impact on our soul. It not only inspires us by acting as a model for contemporary works of art, but also gives an insight into the perennial principles which the artist applied to make this art – values which still form a basis for a valid contemporary artistic expression. This kind of education requires a totally different appreciation from that of viewing so-called modern art – one that is not centred on the art as the work of the individual artist, but on the artist's particular expression of a universal principle.

5. Heritage through architecture

The Islamic world today is finally starting to recognise the true value of the rich heritage it has inherited. The issues of conservation and preservation have become the leading concerns of the day. But one has to ask the following questions: 'By what means do we preserve this inheritance and what extent do we allow it to interact with our so-called modern lifestyles?' Is it enough to have a long distance and comfortable

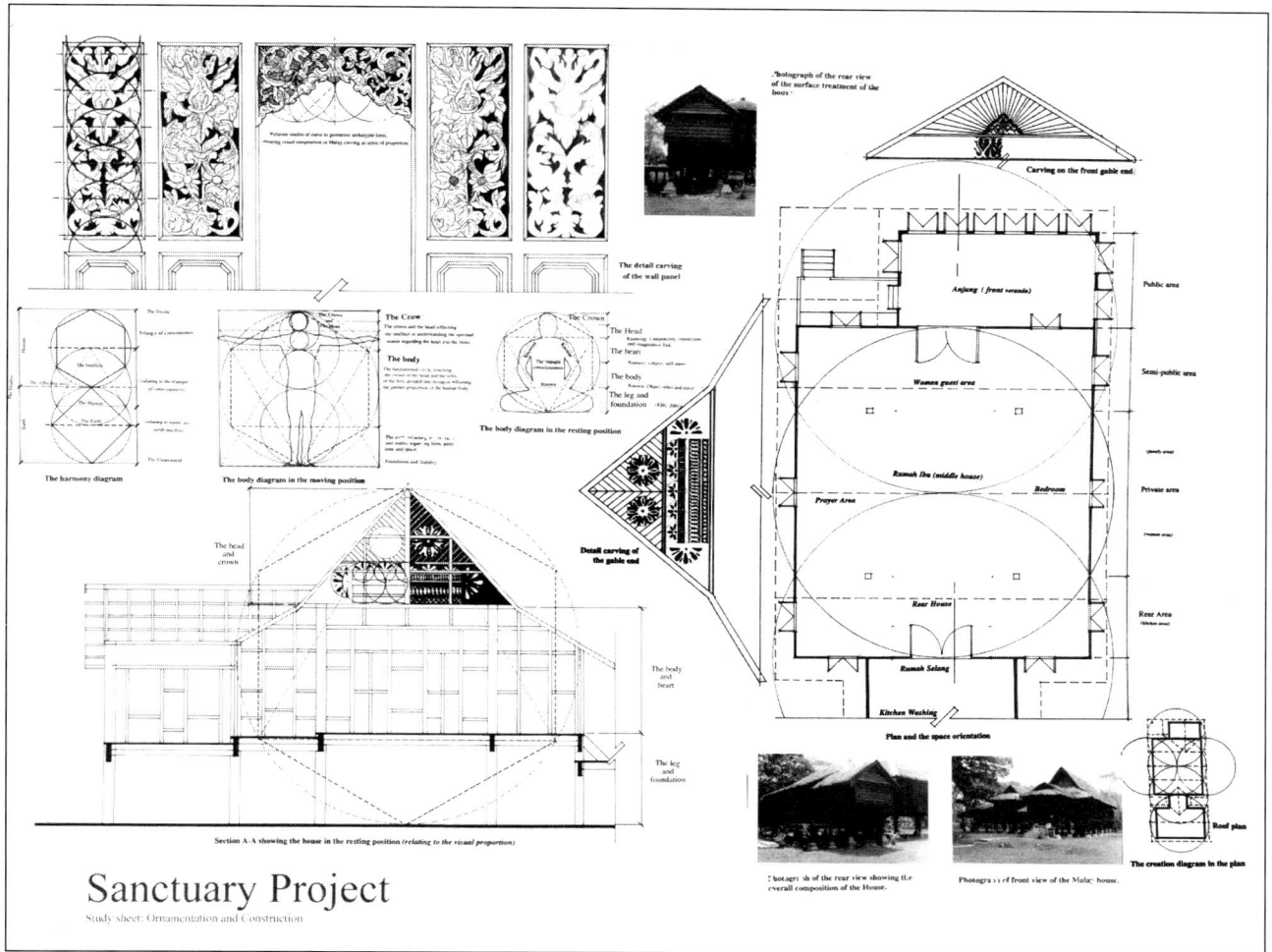

Sanctuary Project
Study sheet: Ornamentation and Construction

relationship with our past heritage, which is a source of communal pride and identity or do we listen to the uncomfortable questions it keeps asking us today? Is this kind of preservation to be in the form of craft workshops and museums?' This last question, unhappily, would mean a fundamental shift in the position of our heritage from a central one in our everyday lives to one consigned to the outer edges, soon to be relegated

Hazman Hazumi: Sanctuary project, 2000–2002.
Reproduced by permission of PSTA.

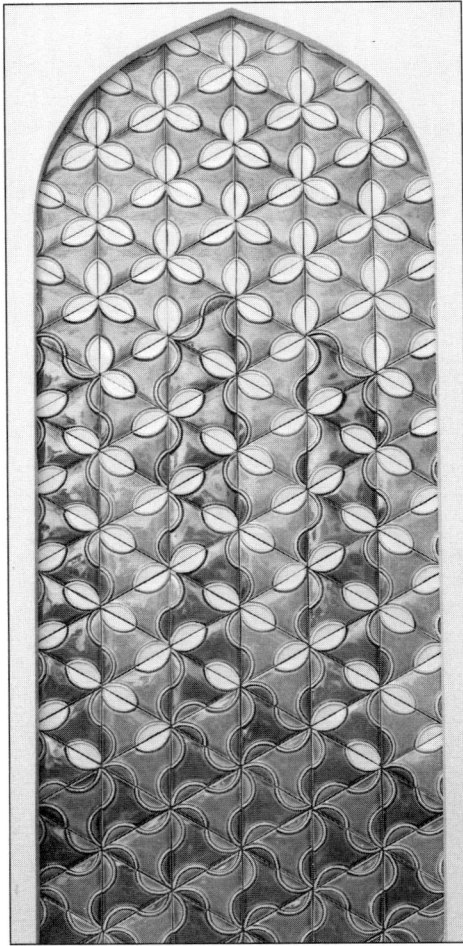

Delfina Bottesini:
Blue ceramic door, 2000–2002.
Reproduced by permission of PSTA.

to the realm of archaeology, folklore and historical-cultural education. This I believe to be a very short-term answer to the problem, an answer that stems from a lack of understanding of the true significance of the arts and crafts in any society.

Craftsmanship should be understood as a process and not a product. It is a process that includes social, economic, cultural and technical dimensions, as well as the spiritual dimension, all of which bind different aspects of the community together. Thus the destruction of craftsmanship does not only have a negative impact on the arts of a civilisation, but also on its general wellbeing. The work of the craftsman cannot be separated from the other aspects of his life and the life of his community. In order to achieve a correct understanding of the arts and architecture of Islam it is important to know that these arts are the outcome of a fulfilled human being; and this fulfilment is the result of an essential harmony between the hand, the heart and the mind. It is because of this understanding that we stress that intellectual and/or aesthetic appreciation of these arts is not enough. The true identity of the artist can only be realised when he fulfils his role as a craftsman; and his means of expression can only be truly valid when it derives from the principle of unity that underlies every aspect of a Muslim's life. The traditional arts of Islam – as indeed the arts of any of the great sacred traditions – were always seen as a reminder of a higher state of being. They are symbols on earth of the heavenly archetype and are thus supports for contemplation. It is this contemplative nature of traditional Islamic art which removes it from the constraints of time and place, and from an understanding of this the contemporary artist can draw, not only physical but also spiritual inspiration, to form a basis for his or her art. These timeless and universal values will truly provide the freedom from social constraints and psychological preoccupations which every artist searches for in his or her work.

HIDDEN DIVERSITY IN THE TRADITIONAL ARTS

Alexander Stoddart

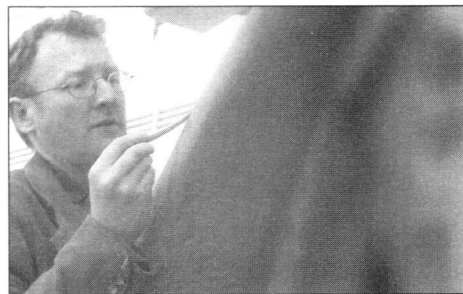

1. Introduction

Alexander Stoddart gave an illustrated talk introduced as 'Hidden Diversity in the Traditional Arts.' No transcript is possible, for the presentation depended on an extemporised, 'vaudeville' style, closely linked to the visual material, which came in fast profusion. Stoddart has, however, provided a reduced account of several of the key points to emerge from his speech, here given in a style fit for reading. There are textual illustrations, some drawn from events subsequent to the conference.

As a central consequence of the Modernist experiment there has arisen in modern culture a profound lack of aesthetic discernment. We live, today, in a world where knowledge of differing styles and manners seems almost to have disappeared and the process – almost the mechanism – that was employed to achieve this ignorance must be recognised as one of the most startling and even sublime developments in the history of Occidental Civilisation. Who could not marvel at the prospect of a major British architect, featured on television recently, mistaking the Parthenon for the Pantheon? Does not the heart race with wonder when Henry Moore is lauded by the contemporary art authorities as a great sculptor in the classical tradition? How could we fail to thrill at the suggestion of a radio musicologist that Claude Debussy was an 'Impressionist' composer? All this unutterable chaos of interpretation derives from one unfortunate sequence of events; the perfectly unique artistic phenomenon, unknown and unanticipated in any epoch in western history, when the thought of a work of art was predicated on the necessity to innovate. This was the essence of

ALEXANDER STODDART

Alexander Stoddart is a Scottish sculptor, born in Edinburgh in 1959. He has been making sculpture and statuary in Paisley, Scotland, for over 20 years. He attended Glasgow School of Art from 1976–1980, Glasgow University from 1980–1983; and afterwards began his career as a sculptor in Paisley in heroic and colossal scales and monumental form. In 2002, Alexander Stoddart completed a schema for the Queen's Gallery at Buckingham Palace.

Alexander Stoddart's works are in his native style of neo-classicism, periodically turning to Heroic Realism for the purposes of historical monuments and symbolic portraiture. He has written extensively on the philosophy of aesthetics and is currently in the early stages of writing a book, entitled "The Metaphysics of Philistinism."

In 1998 Alexander Stoddart was awarded a University Doctorate from the University of Paisley, in 2001 was honoured with the Arthur Ross Award of Classical America for Public Statuary and in 2006 was awarded an Honorary Degree of Doctor of Letters from the University of Glasgow. He is also a member of INTBAU College of Traditional Practitioners (ICTP).

Sandy Stoddart: Lady Elizabeth Bowes-Lyon c. 1920.
Study in plaster of Paris, 2006.

Modernism. In the ensuing perpetual convulse, the constant revolution of that sequence of fifty decades, the divorce hurried through between the individual artist and his predecessors left the latter unobserved and the former unsupported. One attended art-school in the 1970s surrounded by candidates of widely different interests and backgrounds united in one single respect – that they knew not the slightest fact about the art of the past. This, in any age hitherto, would seem to disqualify such an institution as having anything whatsoever to do either with schooling or with art. Today the problem stands compounded.

2. The philistine word

The upshot of the disregard for the art of the past is a contemporary art-world that is unable to discern *difference* in any subtle or fine measure. Traditionally, developments in style in the visual arts proceeded at such a slow pace that the slightest deviation was instantly seen as a kind of outrage – even if it was pleasant to behold. Social ideals of fidelity and loyalty filtered into the artistic domain and one maintained a care for the opinion of one's old master. In time the position of the venerable master would be one's own, and so the callow youth held open a 'diplomatic channel' to his ancient self to come; a kind of 'forward-looking' quite alien to that of a more Blairite tint. So it is that one famous 'modernist' in a time of surviving and vital tradition, Richard Wagner, is especially devoted to the art of several of his precursors; Gluck, Weber and above all Beethoven. The *avant garde*, in the 19th century, was indentified in atavism. Then an artist was expected to have, above all critics, academics and pundits, knowledge of his art in many times, which is to say knowledge of his art *beyond himself.* Now he is a blundering fool, isolated in youth and solipsistic confidence. And there are structures in place to keep him just so.

As powers of representation diminished (powers such as those of drawing above all), so accelerated recourse has been made to that other means of depiction; the crude tool of the word. Schopenhauer has much to say about the verbal utterance appearing in the place of the art-work and a net-work of significant links can be woven from this. The word stands in for the form in so much officially-sanctioned contemporary art (the favoured expression for this is 'text-based art') and it is the very root and branch of what we have come to know and hate as 'conceptual art'. This is, astonishingly, a very accurate title for this kind of activity for, as Schopenhauer adroitly put it, 'The word is the handmaiden of the concept.' This can be the only explanation for the appeal that this kind of art has had in critical circles, for it is an art, born of chatter, which excites others to still more verbiage. Thus it emerges as an art of the social milieu, serving to prime the pump of dialogue, controversy and press excitement. Works of art designed specifically to calm the world – which is to say all the great art of the past – are of no use to the scandal-hungry contemporist kennel. But the yapping has to stop if the viewer of the art-work requires to measure the *differences* between one object and another, and to estimate those qualities that are beyond the powers of language to describe.

Several examples can be provided where a rude 'conceptual' attitude to visual art has shown itself. Once, in the Art Galleries of Paisley, a lady in charge of visual art there (and a known contemporist) took it upon herself in a sort of outburst to let me know in no uncertain terms where her loyalties lay. We were standing at the junction between three rooms in the building, where various paintings were on display. In the largest room works from the 19th and early twentieth centuries were hung, representing a huge diversity of styles, from masters as different as Maurice Grieffenhagen, Sam Bough, Monticelli and George Henry. 'This' the lady announced, making a block gesture with her two hands in the direction of the hall, 'I can accept for what it is.' She then turned to point over toward the second hall, where a small selection of mid-twentieth-century painting was presented. 'I'm not at all keen on this,' said she, leaving poor Sir William Gillies to his plodding greys and dripping Borders all forlorn, together with his fellow cattle in this new-made corral of disdain. Spinning round on her heel, and with a wide sweep of the open palm, the lady now presented the third room; a chilly white apartment, sparsely hung in the manner one might expect. A subtle row of boxes hung from the wall, with some string, if I am not

Sandy Stoddart: Clay model of the Adam Smith statue, Edinburgh. In progress, 2006, with the artist.

Sandy Stoddart: Decorative Capital; Andrea, goddess of courage. Clay model in production, 2006. For a new commercial building in Piccadilly, London. Robert Adam Architects.

mistaken, trailing from one or the other of them. A stripy canvas at the other end of a Yukon of white-wall. Another mess off to the side. 'This', she now block-gestured again, pulling down her brows to mark her seriousness and lowering her vocal tones, 'is what I'm *really* interested in.'

Thus three rooms, filled with an unimaginable variety of subjects, styles, affections, symbolisms, associated triumphs and tragedies, techniques, perspectives and *colours*, had been disposed of in three statements. The key to observing this pantomime lies in the understanding that not a single work had been examined in itself, in silence or compelled deliberation. In fact, the works had been positively *dismissed;* even those enjoying approval! This is a paradigm of the conceptualist approach to the problem of the art-work. It is really a kind of philistinism and I have to admit that it is particularly rife in modern-day Scotland, a country that has had more than its share of art difficulties, largely on account of its love of the word over the image (Reformationism) and its need to deconstruct (Enlightenment).

3. Conceptual and perceptual art

'The broader the statement, the narrower the mind' – a Victorian platitude, but not false. We can see how Conceptualism rose out of a leftist political milieu and how, on the contrary, fine connoisseurship; the dwelling on artistic nicety and the pursuit of the unfathomable beauty has been lent a rightist or Conservative aspect. For as the 'block-denominative' approach leaves two hundred paintings in internal exile, so people can be disposed of in likewise brutal and careless gestures of command under the sway of political *optimism*, which is the essence of leftist thinking. The loss of human life in such contexts is an inevitable accompaniment to the loss of that which makes life bearable; the consolational work of art, appreciated for its infinite curiosities and distracting powers, every one unassailable by the jack-booted word. So it is that one finds oneself often in a sticky situation when protesting one's love of art in leftist social circles. Something betrays one as a deserter from the Dialectic Cause; at the metaphysical level this is simply the visceral detection of the aesthete's less-than-watertight loyalty to the will-to-live.

He is not sporty, enjoys darker rooms than light, and is bookish, perhaps a little limp. He cannot abide rock music. He turns to the art-work for release from life's rascalry and in that turning he immerses himself in an infinity of perceptual wanderings. For the opposite of conceptual art (and few conceptualists even know this) is *perceptual* art; an art, or even simply art itself, to which the bumbling hand-maiden of the *word* is no assistance. True aesthetic experience is felt only when the gag is firmly in place; when the self, and the self's interests, are neither expressed nor accommodated.

With the expansion of theoretical approaches to art under the Modernist *junta*, the unavoidable loss of discernment has deprived countless millions from the birth-right to enjoy a variety of visual experiences. In sculpture this has been particularly evident and nowhere more than in the estimation of those two widely diverging manners known as neo-classicism, and realism. As these two manners are packed together in the single coffin inscribed 'Figurative', so even those who would protest their right still to live and thrive proceed to elevate them on a *pedestal* inscribed 'Figurative'. This is done through a sub-perceptual carelessness of estimation and it is a fundamental error of judgement born of Modernism's atrocities and shocks. American traditionalism is especially guilty of treating traditionalist sculpture as one 'figurative' thing, yet this is only born of innocence. But, as the modern American school of painting known as 'classical realism' divulges in its title, this error indicates a mighty deficit in *sensibility*. For classicism, if it is anything, is a furious and headlong assault on realism. The two only appear united if one views the world from the standpoint of the *abstractionist* or the *brutalist/distortionist. (*The clans Campbell and MacDonald look like one thing, if one's perspective is conditioned by a power completely ignorant of the fundamental opposition between the two Highland administrations.)

Sandy Stoddart: Detail of a herm of Priapus, from the seventh Eclogue of Virgil. Clay model in progress, 2006. For a new building in Vincent Square, London. John Simpson, architect.

4. The decline of visual culture

I have enjoyed, for my own part, a measure of appreciation of my works of sculpture from America such I had never thought to receive. Yet I observe that conceptual thinking (i.e., 'figure-work, *ergo* classical')

Sandy Stoddart: St. Rita of Cascia. Bronze, 2006. Set in the tympanum of a new private chapel in the north of Britain. Craig Hamilton, architect.

infects even this appreciation. Many in the New World assume to set my various works wholesale into a common camp with, say, the late sculptor Frederic Hart. There is often an implicit faith that I will regard Hart's *oeuvre* as contiguous with my own, and regard it with approval. What consternation, then, when I insist upon the fundamental and primal *opposition* between what Hart achieved and what I try to achieve. When I say that I would sooner own and display a work by Donald Judd than one by Hart, there is a terrible stiffening of relations and we move onto other subjects. In any pre-Modernist discussion such a difficulty would never have arisen, for the slow process of cultural development would have clearly articulated the yawning abyss that exists between the two sculptural outlooks and Hart and I would have been presumed to be in *dire enmity*. So it was, indeed, when the young tiros of the British 'New Sculpture' movement of the late 19th century (Thorneycroft, Brock, Frampton, Gilbert, Pomeroy, etc.) set up against the legacy of John Gibson, William Theed and, ultimately, Chantrey. The world of difference between a work like Gilbert's 'Angel of Christian Charity' (Eros, Piccadilly Circus, London), and Gibson's 'Tinted Venus' (Walker Art gallery, Liverpool) was seen and registered. It was a scandal and revolution. Today, the two works are indicated by a block gesture of the hands, and described as 'that', both by people kindly and unkindly disposed to them. Visual culture, then, is in a desperate defile.

Scottish art history tells of a time when the differences between objects in differing styles were understood even at the municipal level. In the 1840s, the City of Glasgow sought to erect a statue of the Duke of Wellington. The commission was given, some say through corruption, to a fashionable Piemontese sculptor resident in London, the Baron Carlo Marochetti. A growing nationalist conscience in Scottish art circles felt it wrong that a national testimonial should go to some sculptor other than a Scot, and a campaign to alert the nation as a whole to the benefits of engaging a native hand was commenced. The controversy reached a height when the London Times reported that, at a City Council meeting, the Baron Marochetti was deemed, by the nationalist side, unsuitable for such a Scottish work insofar as his style descended from the luxurious style of Canova, rather than from the sterner, more chaste style of Thorvaldsen, the latter sculptor (a Dane) being the transcendent inspiration for the entire nascent Scottish School of sculpture. Marochetti's actual manner is not to the point. What is important is that some men in political power in a Scottish City were discussing a manner of art at a level of discernment which we might not be certain to encounter even in academic contexts today. They were demonstrating their knowledge of stylistic nicety and furthermore drawing conclusions of an ethical sort from their disquisitions.

Sandy Stoddart: David Hume statue, Royal Mile, Edinburgh. Bronze, 1996.

Now, Canova and Thorvaldsen are, in many respects, very close. They are both leading neo-classical sculptors, and they were mutually admiring. Yet appreciation and knowledge of their respective works depends on an estimation of their *differences* (if neo-classicism is supposed still to exist), and of their *similarities* (if that style is supposed to be gone). For as similar sculptors they can be packaged into historical storage. When they are seen as *different*, there is then a hint that they assume, once more, a pedagogical role. In short, to relegate these two sculptors to obsolescence they must be treated as one, typical entity. To keep them with us they must be divided as to

'Nicolas Poussin: The Arcadian Shepherds: 'Et in Arcadia Ego' © The Devonshire Collection, Chatsworth. Reproduced by permission of the Chatsworth Settlement Trustees.'

their parts and qualities and from that division so we will learn. Neo-classical sculpture we will know to be returned to us as a working manner when Canovanians are warring with Thorvaldsenians. Taste will have returned and returned amongst artists.

5. Aesthetic objectivity

In my own work, I observe a strict division between the sculptures I make in the various traditional idioms. Heroic realist works stand *opposed to* neo-classical pieces; 'Fairy-realism' *confronts* ecclesiasticism. All my enemies and sadly too many of my supporters, regard the studio as a unified entity – 'full of classical sculpture'. Yet architects in the traditionalist movement enjoy a better appreciation of difference of manner, when a gothic scheme of works is seen on a desk next to an Arts-and-Crafts or a classical… or even a neo-classical. It is imperative, incidentally, that traditionalist practices learn to design modernist pavilions for erection in large country estates, as hermitages, or curious sequestered freaks, or *follies* – redolent of a distant, helplessly barbaric, heroic age.

Hitherto, in the main body of the twentieth (the last) century, the philosophers attempted to change the world. The point, however, is to *interpret* it. For despite the concerted efforts of the Hegelians of the last century not to change, but indeed to do away with the world, the world, astonishingly, continued as perplexing and umbriferous as before and men still could be found who measured in the Imperial scale. Art is not of this world, but as the philosophers of better times well understood, rather more indicative of somewhere else, and this is surely why the activists of contemporism take such exception to it, since they cannot imagine themselves as *not being*. Aesthetic experience provides a floating platform of objectivity from whence the world can be observed and from that point reality is easily seen – easily fathomed. But there is something also to be observed at the other side of this platform, this 'magic carpet'. To comprehend that 'beyond' you have to attend to the differences between subtle passages in works of art and music, such as are called 'passages' for no idle reason. But then you will have entered an engulfing firmament, never to return.

BUILDING & PLACES

ROBERT ADAM

Robert Adam was born in 1948 and trained at the University of Westminster and in 1973 won a Rome Scholarship. He has practised in the city of Winchester since 1977. His projects in the UK and abroad include major private houses, extensions to historic buildings and public and commercial buildings. He has a long history of work on speculative housing and masterplanning and founded the Popular Housing Group in 1995 and International Network for Traditional Building, Architecture & Urbanism from 2000. Adam's work is widely published, broadcast and exhibited. He has written numerous historical, critical and theoretical papers and published a book on classical design and a children's book on architecture. He lectures widely and has undertaken lecture tours of the USA and Russia.

TRADITIONAL ARCHITECTURE: WHY COMMUNITIES NEED IT

Robert Adam

1. Introduction

We can look at architecture in two ways: as a piece of technology, a 'machine for living'; or as just one part of many things that go to make up a society. If we look at architecture as one of the pieces of the huge jigsaw that makes up a society, it must be bound up with the history, activities and symbols peculiar to that society – in other words its customs and traditions. Once you accept that architecture is a part of the unique identity of a society or community, you have to accept that it is a part of the traditions of that community.

In the twentieth century, however, a great deal of effort was expended trying to cleanse architecture of this messy association with the past. Custom and tradition were thought to be old fashioned and so not subject to the intellectual rigour of the scientific progress that was changing the world and would make it a better place. Tradition and custom were not modern and so were not seen as authentic to the modern condition. A new modern principle was required that would transcend local differences of history and give an objective and universal standard for the improvement and authenticity (or, as it was sometimes called, honesty) of architecture. This principle was supplied either by comparing buildings with machines or (in a similar vein) by defining society – and so its architecture – by the latest technological developments (much as Karl Marx had defined society by its means of production). Technology was thought to be free of the chains of history, custom and tradition and so modern technology would be authentic to its period and represent pure and scientific progress. This, it was thought, would be a suitable model for the new architecture of the twentieth century.

This is the current architectural philosophy and is known as Modernism.

2. Is the new technology pure progress?

It might, therefore, be a useful start to an examination of tradition in architecture to take a brief look at the role of technology in society and architecture. Just how appropriate is this model? Is technological advance pure progress untrammelled by custom and history and driven only by its own dynamic?

Here are two examples of new technology.

The Eurostar runs, as do most of the world's railways, on a rail gauge that is pretty much the gauge of the horse-drawn railway at Killington colliery where Stevenson developed the first locomotives. That is 4ft 8 and 3/8inches.

The keyboard used for computers – the QWERTY layout – was designed in America in 1873 to slow typists down to avoid the collision of key bars.

Attempts to inject pure progress into both of these apparently obsolete features were tried and failed. The fact is that technological progress is not and cannot be independent of the society it serves. It was pointless changing millions of miles of rails and retraining millions of typists for an ideal of pure progress. Modern railways and modern computers – and most other objects that we make and use – are a product of society first and technology second.

This is not just, as with the examples quoted, a case of what is practical. It is also aesthetic and cultural. I will just give one example. In the 1950s and 60s the ceramic industry was in crisis. It was clear that plastics were – or soon would be – a superior material for crockery: cheap, lightweight, virtually unbreakable, and resistant to chemicals and heat. The crisis never occurred. Eating was an aesthetic and ritualised affair which was peculiar to our culture and not to be spoilt with something that felt wrong – however technically superior.

Designed to slow typists down.

Modern product, traditional design.

Technology could be used to improve the manufacture of the product but not the status and ritual qualities of the product.

3. Culture and technology

So we can see that even technology, that god of Modernism, is dependant on the culture it serves. It responds to its own technical and practical system of customary use. Most critically, it too responds to customs and traditions and has no inevitable technical or aesthetic outcome. Artefacts develop with society and every artefact carries with it the history of its technical evolution in that society.

Architecture and building are, of course, very complex artefacts with origins deep in prehistory. They have a much longer technological evolution than the railway and the computer and a similar technical lifespan to ceramics. The relationship between buildings and the history, customs and traditions of the people that use them is bound to be complex and deep rooted – both technologically and culturally.

The confusion created in architecture by the Modernist misunderstanding of technology is best seen in attitudes to prefabrication.

Prefabrication was, and still is, seen as the Holy Grail of technological progress in building – particularly housing. This is seen as proper technical progress and so, in the eyes of the modernists, it would lead, as day follows night, not just to better and more efficient building but also to modernist design. But like all technology, society (or the market driven by society) rules and technology follows. In Japan, where prefabricated housing has reached its current peak of technological development the result is, more often than not, traditional.

4. Architecture and tradition

Nothing better than housing shows us how we really feel about architecture. There are more houses than any other type of building. Houses are bought by ordinary people, according to preference. Everyone understands housing and its use and symbolism are transparently determined by the social customs and traditions of society.

Prefabricated Japanese speculative house.

Most popular house type in UK. From *Kerb Appeal,*
Popular Housing Forum, 1998.

A recent survey of attitudes to the appearance of housing in England and Wales by the Popular Housing Group came up (rather as a by-product of the research) with an interesting insight into attitudes to exterior house design. (Interiors were not part of the research.)

In order to find the key concepts in the choice of housing, subjects were asked to choose a card of types of housing design. Overtly modernist selections of houses were only chosen by 1.5% of the sample. They were variously described as 'garages', 'nuclear power stations' or 'factories'. On the other hand, the speculative-traditional housing selection was chosen by about 40%. A selection of conventional speculative traditional houses was chosen by about 30% and the architecture designed traditional houses by 25%. (As a check a milder modernist selection were only chosen by about 3%.) As a reader you may or may not like the most popular houses, but you would, in common terminology call them 'traditional'. Indeed, when the research yielded its key concepts, three of the four aesthetic criteria were 'character', 'individual' and 'traditional'.

While the popular choices were clearly traditional, architects here will confirm that most of them are not authentic – that is they are not accurate versions of the historic types that they seek to emulate. Nor are they in any way constructionally authentic. Indeed, the modern house, whatever it looks like, is a product of a modern building industry and the use of new materials and techniques is in accordance with economy and regulation rather than historic authenticity.

The focus group discussion on these houses was revealing. The members of the groups, properly constructed across socio/economic lines, were not stupid. They knew full well that (to use a semi-humorous industry term) 'gob-ons' such as half-timbering were not authentic. They were to them, rather, reminders, souvenirs or mementos of something desirable

5. Authenticity and tradition

Clearly complete authenticity was not necessary to many of these people to make the associations and symbolic gestures required. But buildings can be authentic in many different ways. This search for authenticity and its companions, honesty and truth, has dogged architectural debate since the renaissance and, in particular, since the gothic revival.

Authenticity to the modern age is the driving force of Modernism. Only those things that appear to be modern are considered to be authentic for contemporary society. In this way history, custom and tradition are excluded. This view extends to lifestyle. So, if you design in an historic style it is believed, cynically, that you should live in an historic manner. To design in a Georgian style, therefore, implies that you use oil lights and hang criminals for theft. To do otherwise would be dishonest or inauthentic. Modern life, to take this theory to its logical conclusion, can only be authentically lived in a house which consists of materials and technology exclusive to a modern age. This is patently ridiculous if not impossible but it is an idea that still has common currency in design circles.

Ordinary people, on the other hand, always sensible, see no contradiction between new technology and historic design. They have no problem with owning a new car and a new but traditional house – each is a product of its own technological evolution, has its own technical traditions and responds appropriately to the traditions of society. If you accept that history, custom and tradition are an authentic part of modern society, then you must accept that their incorporation into architecture (or any other part of life) is an authentic, honest or true reflection of modern society.

But what of construction? Is it necessary to build something in the way it was originally built in order to be authentically traditional? Some people, I think, hold this view. This is, in my opinion, really another version of the way-of-life theory. It confuses two issues: it is quite correct to criticise those who abandon old and tried methods of building just because they are old, as the lessons of history and good techniques can be lost; to go to the extreme and insist that traditional design must be built in an entirely historic way is both impossible and unnecessary (furthermore it is un-historical). Tradition is and always

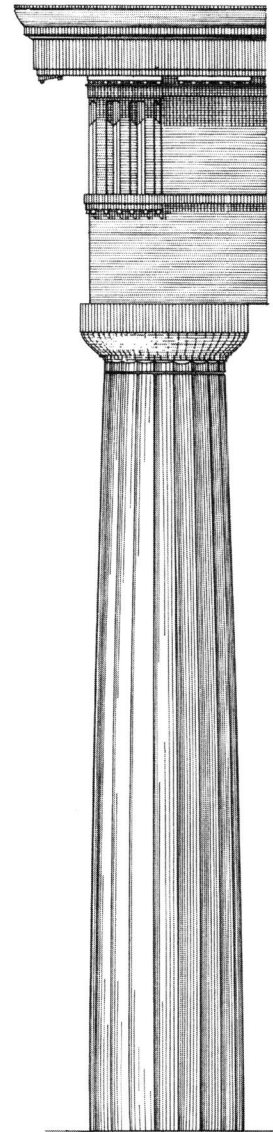

Doric Column. From *Classical Architecture, a complete handbook,* Robert Adam, 1990.

Millennium Pavilion.

has been largely symbolic. Again, ordinary people understand this – as seen with the survey. They might be able to get a better version of their traditional 'gob-ons', but they fully understand that they do not have to be exactly the same as the things they symbolise.

Which leads us to the much more difficult issue of aesthetic authenticity. To those of us trained in classical design, inaccuracy in detail is both common and painful. We will always try and design in a way that we believe is aesthetically authentic – it is our struggle and our duty. As we have seen, however, there is a hard-to-define threshold between inaccuracy in detail and the way a thing is made and what it does. If a Doric column was, historically, stone and supported a roof, is a Doric column made of plaster that supports nothing and is attached to a wall authentic? Or, put another way, if you tap a column and find it hollow, is this column authentic? Many people believe it isn't.

6. Facsimile versus tradition

This problem takes us to the fine line between historicism – the desire to produce a facsimile – and tradition – the continuation of the historic activities and symbols peculiar to a society. These are not necessarily the same thing. In the difference between historicism and tradition, I believe, lies the key to progress and invention in traditional design. There are different types of aesthetic authenticity. I use two of my own buildings to illustrate the point.

In the entrance to the new Sackler Library in Oxford, the columns and entablature are both stone and of the precise proportions of the temple of Apollo at Bassae. They are, in an historicist sense, authentic. This was to make a specific reference to the Ashmolean Museum by C.R. Cockerell (to which this building is an extension) where the Ionic Order from the same temple is used in the portico. This is both historicist and traditional.

In the millennium garden temple for Lord Sainsbury, the columns may be stone and the capitals bronze but there is no entablature at all and the capitals have been designed without an abacus. The copper dome is held up by tapered stainless steel rods and braced with stainless steel wires. We know that the ancients wanted to make domes that appeared to float, but could not. We can. This is clearly in the classical tradition but it could not have been done in the past. It uses modern materials and the latest understanding of statics (the engineering is also pioneering and had to be calculated from first principles). This is traditional but not historicist.

Neither of these buildings is wrong, both are modern and both are in the classical tradition. But one is made of an authentic historic material and authentic proportions and the other is not. One only adds to classical architecture numerically, the other adds a new variation (which may or may not be of any long term significance at all). Tradition, being symbolic rather than imititative, is the medium by which historic design types that have a particular symbolic relevance for a community can change. Tradition is a medium for change – change that does not seek to disrupt the equilibrium of society.

Sackler Library.

TRADITION TODAY: TRADITIONAL URBANISM

Léon Krier

LÉON KRIER

Léon Krier was born in 1946 in Luxembourg but settled in Provence after living in England for twenty years. He is internationally known as a renovator of traditional architecture and urbanism. His theories form part of the urban development recommendations of the OECD and the European Union. They have been widely applied in the United States, via the New Urbanism movement, and, more recently, in Europe. Léon Krier is a personal adviser to the Prince of Wales, for whom he masterplanned the new town of Poundbury in Dorset in the United Kingdom, and is currently masterplanning the new growth area of Newquay in Cornwall, UK.

1. Introduction

Ten years ago, the then academic board of the burgeoning Prince of Wales Institute, 'in clausura' in an Oxford College, were pondering how this baby should best be named. During the two days proceedings, an unlikely coalition of characters, ranging from Christopher Alexander to John Thompson gradually united in their opposition to the term 'traditional,' which I had proposed.

I suggested that not only did 'traditional' best sum up HRH's environmental message, but equally it would safeguard the young institute against likely modernist take-overs and foreseeable subversions. I ended up in a minority of one. The tragic waste of resources and careers which went on at Gloucester Gate for so many years and directorships, could probably not be avoided.

Despite the turmoil, the ground was being readied for what is now possible, i.e. offering alternative choices in architecture and urbanism.

Negotiating a breathing space within a modernist cultural hegemony (and the Palace's natural political opportunism) was necessarily a labourious process. I want to comfort myself with the thoughts, that none of us here wants to replace the modernist dictatorship with other forms of ideological hegemony, be they of a traditional nature. I wanted to keep Poundbury free of modernist interventions, not out of a pursuit of purity but to prove the point that democracy can produce a coherent piece of traditional townscape. Twenty years ago, we were told that it was impossible from a theoretical or a practical point of view; now, that it is not only working, but having become a broad success and even a government model for development, the old objectors come asking, 'Will you ever allow "contemporary" style buildings?' To which I routinely reply, 'Do you ask Lord Foster whether one day he will put tiled roofs on his buildings?'

Democracy is after all supposed to be a game of reciprocal toleration. We will have mixed style traditional developments, if and when modernists are prepared to play the game, to share their cake as well as ours.

2. Defending traditional urbanism

It is evidently a gross but tenacious fallacy to believe that there could be such a thing as a 'democratic style.' Democracy is about plural choices and it is us alone who are introducing that issue into the present cultural agenda. So far modernists are not yet prepared to practice the openness they so regularly demand of us. For a long while

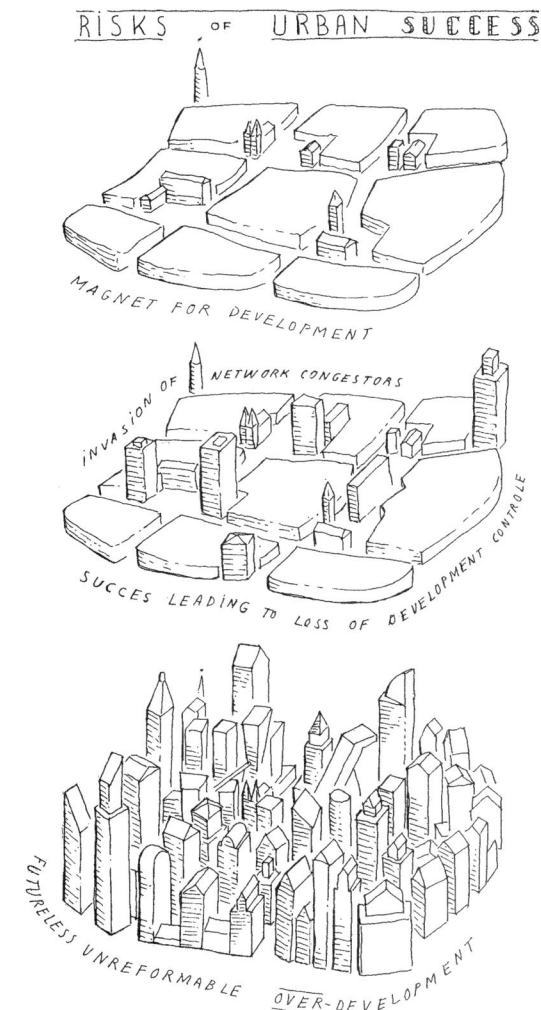

The Pink House, Poundbury, by Nigel Anderson of Robert Adam. Architects Masterplanner Léon Krier. Image Matthew Hardy.

ARCHITECTURAL TUNING OF
URBAN COMPOSITION
⟨ vernacular & classical ⟩

vernacularissimus
AUSTERITY VERNACULAR

vernacular & classical
CULTURAL APOGEE

CLASSICISSIMUS
IMPERIAL CARNIVAL CLASSICISM

House on Chaseborough Square, Poundbury.
Masterplanner Léon Krier. Image Richard Ivey.

the Palace objected to Prince Charles espousing what they thought was a single architectural style, forgetting that traditional architecture and urbanism embrace all architectural styles, including modernist styles. This very broad cultural, technological and geographic plurality needed so badly to be defended by Prince Charles because it had no high-ranking champion left, except him.

For over six years, following the announcement of Poundbury, Prince Charles had to brave mountains of abuse and lies. I lost most of my architect 'friends'. I had some very powerful and courageous clients before, but none was prepared to pay that sort of price for what seemed a reasonable undertaking.

The traditional agenda needed a powerful and independent protector exactly because it has been so radically cornered and aggressively excluded from architectural education and institution patronage.

The case for architectural democracy and plurality has not been won; it has only just been formulated and announced. It will take another two generations before we will get to a routine multi-party practice and schooling in these matters.

3. Timeless and traditional?

Another enduring fallacy is to consider traditional architecture and urbanism as 'historic' and ipso facto as dated and discardable.

We propose instead to range traditional architecture within the realm of technology, with the study and practice of techniques, timeless

I am a house

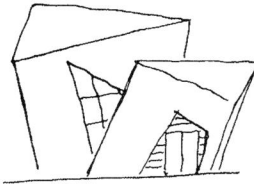

Call me a house

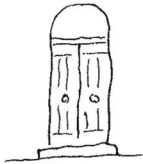

I am a window

Call me a window

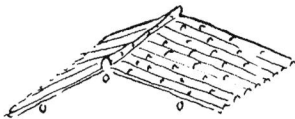

I am a house-door

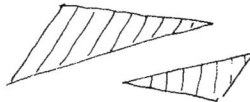

Call me a house-door

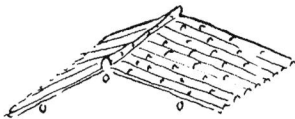

I am a roof

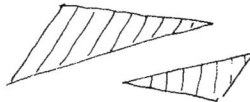

Call me a roof

techniques of settling and building in accordance with conditions of nature and cultures, with geography and climate.

Before that will be possible even the most punctilious traditional architects have to live with a degraded building practice, with an

Market day in Pummery Square, Poundbury. Masterplanner Léon Krier. Image Richard Ivey.

House in Woodlands Crescent, Poundbury by Ben Pentreath. Masterplanner Léon Krier. Image Richard Ivey.

over-complicated building legislation and bureaucracy which render buildings fragile, expensive and short-lived. Most of our buildings, independent of their style, are today in fact little more than full-size models. Whatever their appearance, they are often deconstructed typologically, structurally, and aesthetically. To get to a saner building construction will take a lot of undoing, but to do that, modernist blinkers have to come off first.

A last point: I hope we will be able to face the problems of scale and size, which independent of style issues, affect the quality of cities, buildings and landscapes. Oversized buildings, whether skyscrapers, landscapers or underground-scrapers, necessarily overburden and congest urban networks. Corbusier was right. If you want oversized buildings in the short or long run, you will not have traditional cities.

Single use functional zoning and oversized buildings are products of the same de-humanizing ideologies. They are usually related. There is no historical fate in these matters, nor any irreversibility. With our personal choice of architecture and urbanism, we either support the consolidation of mass-society or help to consolidate and construct a society of individuals. There is little middle ground left. The 'long emergency' announced by J.H. Kunstler will corner us is we do not prepare for it in advance.

Houses in Pendruffle Lane, Poundbury.
Masterplanner Léon Krier. Image Richard Ivey.

Poundbury Stores, Pummery Square, Poundbury.
Affordable housing over a small supermarket.
Masterplanner Léon Krier. Image Richard Ivey.

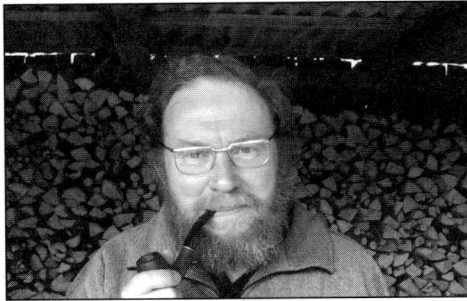

Dynamics of Nature in Buildings

Hans Kolstad

Hans Kolstad

Hans Kolstad is a philosopher. He was born in 1952 in Norway. He is a doctor of philosophy (University of Oslo, 1996) and has a French D.E.A.-degree from the University of Strasbourg (1984). During the last 10 years, he has published more than 20 books on philosophy, literature and art. Particularly, he has been writing on French philosophers such as Descartes, Pascal, Rousseau, Montesquieu, Bergson, Gabriel Marcel and Emmanuel Levinas. He is also the editor of the collected works of Plato in Norway. He has for several years particularly been working with the subject of the philosophy of nature. Since 1996, he has presided over an annual seminar on the philosophy of nature in Oslo. Currently, he is living in Denmark and working as an author.

1. Introduction

Norway has a rich architectural tradition going back hundreds of years when it comes to buildings constructed of wood. Many of these buildings have been carefully preserved either in purpose-built museums or privately. Norwegians today do, however, display a paradoxical attitude towards this tradition. On the one hand they show their appreciation and respect for traditional architecture by placing it in museums, on the other hand; they have a tendency to reject it as part of modern society and culture when it comes to designing and building something new. In contrast to tradition, all forms of modernistic experiments are now welcomed – and in certain situations it is even forbidden to copy old traditional designs. The result is an ever increasing modern architecture which compared to that of the past is aesthetically limited.

Examples of this can be more clearly seen in the central and more culturally historical parts of Norway such as Gudbrandsdalen – an area just under 3 hours drive north of Oslo. Although much of the old architecture has been preserved, one can find, in some cases, next to or just a few meters away, the most awkward attempts at meaningless concrete constructions which, to put it bluntly, actually offends both the eyes and the consciousness. Cultural awareness, in these cases, seems to be less than zero.

The desire for anything modern has been a disaster for traditional architecture in Norway. As early as the 19th century some of the most beautiful Norwegian buildings were demolished or sold – works which today are considered part of the European civilisation's cultural monuments; such as the stave churches. This still continues today. Although the existence of the traditional is tolerated, it is not, however, accepted that this should have any influence or play a functional role. It may be beautiful to look at, but we do not want it brought into our daily existence.

What does it mean if the traditional is excluded from our daily lives, and what are the consequences for us living with this new architecture? I would like to now explore some of these consequences in more detail, especially some consequences which the rupture with traditional architecture has upon the human mind, the nature and the society in general.

2. Interaction between nature and architecture

It should have been an important moment in history when mankind vacated their caves and started building separate dwellings for human occupation. It can be seen as significant that man had built himself protection from what was a dangerous and threatening nature. It can also be seen as symbolic that man has held up his hand to nature, saying: 'Here, but no further' – this is where the domain of man begins.

If one looks closer at this man-made symbol, it is obvious that it was still part of the nature which discontinuance it should represent. The civilization did not create steel and glass constructions at once, but collected the materials from nature. The first human being sought protection from nature through nature itself. In this way a tradition of craftsmanship came into existence which through thousands of years worked alongside and in tact with nature, thereby creating by listening to nature.

For a long period, architecture did not depart from nature. It is a paradox that whilst wanting protection by building permanent constructions that would withstand the unpredictable forces of nature, with constructions that barred nature from man, the connection was so strong that on certain terms man moved some of nature back into

Figure 1: Farmyard from Aakre in Bondalen.

Figure 2: Farmyard from Skjaak.

the house. In this way it is characteristic that the first big architectural period in modern times – the Baroque – is also the period where one started to cultivate flowers indoors: The Baroque period – could be said to be the period of the pot plants. Inside flowers functioned as a substitution for closeness to the real nature and as a way of breaking down the barriers between man and nature. This could in a symbolic and concrete way be illustrated by the coloured leaded glass window which with its fused colours gives a sense of no clear demarcations rather an interplay between the outside and indoors.

In a similar way one can understand the modern human being's focus on feeling content around the fire place in the house. It is as if, still not quite free of his obsession with nature, man has to bring into the lounge a last reminder of the open-air fire from primitive times. But that which used to have a function has today become a purely atmospheric phenomenon.

The interaction between architecture and nature is obvious within Norwegian farm traditions. In particular this can be seen when it comes to the positioning of the houses on the terrain. The confident and superb way this has been done gives a sense of admiration. The building plot was left in its natural state and in addition the houses interact with the contours of the landscape in a harmonious way – without competing with them, but at the same time making it clearly apparent that this is man's creation in nature (see figs 1 and 2).

Looking at these houses – one can see that they have been constructed in timber, either by joining logs horizontally or by raising a framework. It is especially the framework itself which mirrors nature: the row of up-right timbers is like a picture of birch forest with its proud and upright trees (see figs 3, 4, 5 and 6).

The similarity with nature can also be seen in the ornamentation. The main room of the house – the sitting room – was traditionally decorated with a beautiful design of gallery posts and doorframes and often with carved (vine) foliage, the movement they portray is a copy of nature's own; it is the dynamics of nature which has been transferred into the houses and in doing so, gives them life (see fig. 7).

These traditions go back as far as the Middle Ages, and despite outside influences as, for example, in the Renaissance and the Baroque, this craftsmanship could still be seen way into the 18th century in Norway when the first rationalisation of architecture occurs.

By putting such a great emphasis on decorations and by imitating nature, one could be tempted to presume that the man-made was perceived as fulfilment of nature. Man protected himself from nature by exceeding nature in beauty. He started to see nature as something that was incomplete and in someway less real because it was dangerous and unpredictable. The man-made, on the other hand, was perfect and complete. Only by and through man could nature begin to realize itself. So, in man one finds the platonic idea of an ideal nature of which the exterior nature is but a pale image.

How far one is removed from this thought, is illustrated in the following photographs.

This wooden house (fig. 8) is implanted in nature, but the latter is a coincidental frame – in relation to the sensibility of older times, it represents a break between architecture and nature. Although, the houses are constructed of wood and situated in large gardens – they are not intended to be a perfection of the perceivable nature. The houses absorb nature whilst at the same time pushing it away.

Figure 3: Farmyard from Skjaak.

Figure 4: Farmbuildings from Øygarden at Sjaak.

Figure 5: Farmbuildings from Berge at Rauland.

Figure 6: Farmbuildings from Rauland.

The interplay between nature and man is today in many ways regarded as an anachronism. The architects no longer take nature as a starting point for their own work. Rather the opposite; they are seeking to carry out their own ideas which are on a collision course with nature, i.e. by eliminating and removing every element in the architecture of which it is a reminder. Here formal lines, concrete surfaces and artificially produced building materials are cultivated – often with little sense when it comes to matching the individual elements. In the work of many architects in Norway today we have an impression of a desire to create something permanent and unalterable in contrast with the constantly changing nature.

The tendency to break with nature does not only show itself in the urban environment but also in the countryside, particularly in relation to old houses and courtyards. It is, for example, quite normal in Norway to build cabins both in the forest and in the mountains. These cabins have a long cultural tradition, representing copies of small and seasonal mountain farms. Modern cabins have nothing to do with this tradition: they are being built as if they were located in towns. The result is not houses in the real sense of the word but small mountain towns which only lack the tarmacked avenues in order to be what they were meant to be: towns (see figs 9, 10, and 11).

It was perhaps to be expected that modern buildings respecting ecological principles should represent a renewal of traditional architecture and a new sensibility towards nature. In Norway, the ecological thought is very firmly rooted which explains the interest, for instance, in new sources of energy in order to heat the buildings. One such new form of energy could be in harnessing the warmth in the earth instead of electricity and oil. It is, nevertheless, a fact that ecological considerations of this kind seldom go along with any new awareness for traditional architecture as such, nor does it lead to a greater respect for nature. Buildings constructed on ecological principles answer to economic considerations, but are often deprived of other perspectives. They are often equally poor in their architectural form as with any other modern construction. What is a paradox is

Figure 7: Farmyard from Tofte farm at Dovre.

that we can still find buildings which benefit from alternative forms of energy, but which are constructed out of material originating from the last parts of the Norwegian primeval forests. Awareness of one thing does not necessarily lead to awareness of another.

A new tendency within the ecological movement is based on the use of straw together with concrete elements as material used in the constructions. This means that the buildings are made out of materials without any synthetic additives, which makes the buildings more acceptable from the point of view of health. Such materials are also cheap and provide good insulation. This last point is of significant importance in a country with a cold climate such as Norway. Despite these advantages, the use of straw-based materials has nevertheless not been successful. In the last 15 years only a few houses in Norway have been built using these principles. Perhaps this is the exception which proves the general rule of an actual architectural practice hostile to the Norwegian nature.

In this way, all buildings are being uniformed and homogenized. Another consequence is that they are globalized. There is no longer

Figure 8: Building at Lillehammer designed by the architectural firm Diva.

Figure 8: Mountain cabin at Beitostølen.

Figure 10: 'Mountain towns' at Beitostølen.

a difference between a small village in a Norwegian mountain valley and a modern town anywhere else on the planet. Together with the uniformity of so many other things; such as clothes, music and food etc., it is this qualitative narrowing which is the underlying force in a civilization which is becoming more and more impoverished.

3. The threat to human consciousness

What are the consequences of such a narrowing for the human being in direct terms?

Thanks to the French philosopher Henri Bergson (1889–1941) we have got a renewed view of the meaning of the dynamic in the consciousness (Bergson [1]). The deeper consciousness is life, movement, creation, freedom, whereas the part of the consciousness which is turned towards the outer world consist of layers of stiffened forms; conventions, habits. Such rigid, static and mechanical forms play a decisive role in the human being's practical functions. But at the same time they act as a covering of the real life, i.e. life's own creative force. It would, in other words, be totally wrong to consider the rigid forms that the consciousness presents in day-to-day life to be the only life of the consciousness.

The task of philosophy is to recapture the spontaneous contact with the deeper part of reality and in this contact nature plays an essential role. In nature one finds laid down a dynamic in forms and creative power which is intimately tied to the effort of the consciousness and it is because of this that closeness to nature and being together with it represents an extension and enrichment of the human consciousness.

In the same way will the traditional craftsmanship within wooden architecture, which is founded on interplay between nature and culture and sees architecture as perfectionism of nature, address the deeper layers of the consciousness and result in an enrichment of these. The attraction of the dynamic and living that this craftsmanship has on the human being is to be understood on these premises.

Within the winding lines of architecture the consciousness rediscovers itself: The architecture grips us according to Bergson by the rhythmic movement that we feel we can see in the organisational structure of the buildings. On the other hand, the fact that consciousness is pure movement and rhythm itself, explain why the consciousness opens up for the architecture. Architecture understood as rhythmic movements reflects thus not only the outer reality, but moves directly into the soul which it captivates and spellbinds.

Here the approach of the architect is that of the artist. The rhythm in the piece of art makes the onlooker live in harmony with the object; the work consumes us and its rhythm becomes our whole thought and will. In this way the art has a hypnotic effect on the mind. Poetry, music and the visual arts, the first two by their regular rhythms, the last by its repeated symmetrical shapes, exert a sleepy effect on the mind which forgets itself and totally opens up to the intuition conveyed by the artist. Such an experience can vary in intensity – it depends on to what degree our everyday activities have been shut out and how the mind has been programmed to reflect the feeling which the artist is indicating. This type of communication in art – the different shades, the words or the lines – have based on this theory the task of being similar to a calming and soothing injection for the common sense so that it does not resist when the artist's intuition is communicated to the receiver.

This can also be applied to architecture. In architecture, right in the middle of this gripping immobility, certain effects related to those of the rhythm can be recaptured. The symmetry of shapes, the unlimited repetition of the same architectural motif, leads to our powers of observation swinging from the same to the same and enable us to break away from those continual changes which in our daily lives always bring us back to the consciousness regarding our own personality. Just the slightest hint of an idea, however small, will then be enough to fill our whole soul.

But when architecture in this way communicates to us, grips us, even rocks us to sleep in order to give us the architect's vision and will – what else can it mean but that the massive – the static – becomes transparent? With this transparency the substantial and weighty are neutralised: behind the massiveness of architecture something light and transient opens up which in a way dominates the materialistic and

Figure 11: Mountain cabin at Eidsbugarden.

Figure 12: Cabin at Portør designed by Knut Knutsen.

sets the soul into movement. This movement consists of the interplay between an exterior reality and a consciousness phenomenon.

It is the stiff and massive which lead to a narrowing of self-awareness. It threatens the consciousness – with stagnation, extinguishment and rigidity. Examples of this can be found in working life where free creativity and dynamics often have been replaced by conformity, authority and repetition.

Modern architecture with its geometrical straight-lined shapes and the heavy concrete blocks which appear and feature in people's everyday lives, fulfill the same function as repetition and roles within the work place. They curtail man and accustom the consciousness to living in the static rather than in the dynamic. Perhaps did Goethe anticipate modern architecture on this point when he characterized architecture as 'frozen music'?

The consequences of this architectural rigidity of the consciousness are huge. For one thing, they threaten the consciousness itself. It also threatens nature. In this context, I am not so much thinking about the destruction of nature these massive buildings cause, nor am I thinking about the destruction of the aesthetical aspect of experiencing nature that the lack of interplay between architecture and nature in modern architecture causes, but rather the importance on being at one with nature and the understanding of its importance for man. In modern architecture one is made insensitive to nature. Insensitivity will finally become indifference. The debate concerning the development of Oslo City has now come so far that green areas are seen as something messy and out of place rather than something valuable that should be preserved. Some people have even been heard to say that no town is perfect as long as it still maintains its last bit of nature. The question has also been raised as to why it should be important to protect trees – because sooner or later they will die anyway. Why not just get on with building in their place and do it sooner rather than later?

It is rather unfortunate that such thoughts also permeate society as a whole. The work place with its routines and clichés effects man in narrowing ways so that he can easier fit into a mould and thereby be

Figure 13: Church at Holmenkollen, Oslo, designed by Arne Sødal, built 1986.

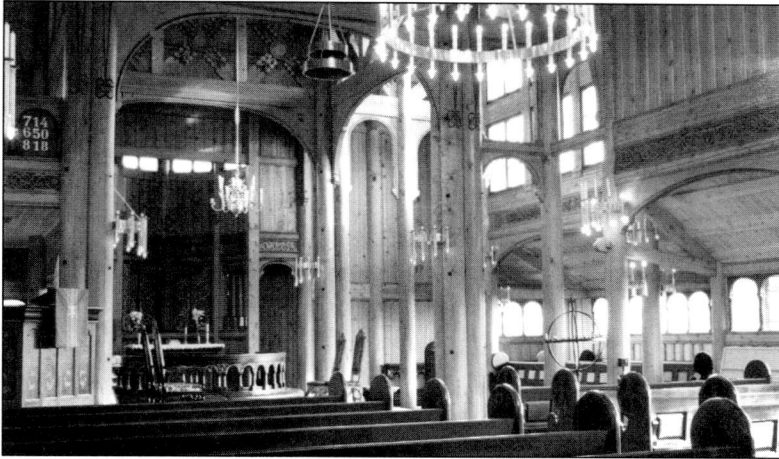

Figure 14: Church at Holmenkollen, (interior).

easier controlled and manipulated and this is exactly how the static architecture affects man in his everyday life. The large concrete blocks, the human hatching boxes, the production units for little battery hens, remind man of an established social order. He begins to think in formal grids and views himself as a small mechanical piece in the machinery. As we all know, it is easier to deal with the square, than what is round; that which has no beginning or end. This is a threat to democracy. A lot of modern architecture – that which cultivates static shapes and geometry – are more than just signs and symbols of a fascist society. Through its suggestive powers it gives the consciousness a feeling of the hopelessness and non-importance of the little man when facing the order of society at large.

4. Defying modern architectural practice and town planning
Leon Krier's article 'Contemporary Perspectives' [2] reminds us of an important point: Buildings and towns are not pieces of art; they are practical answers to practical problems. Traditionalism here goes hand in hand with what is purposeful. Traditional architecture and town planning gives us a practical approach, and this is exactly why they constitute a tradition.

One of Norway's foremost architects, Knut Knutsen (1903—1969), once said that one ought to break with the view that sees architecture as an expression of the leading thoughts and ideas of a certain period. Architecture does not serve the materials and neither should they serve the ideas. Architecture exists for the purpose of the unchangeable human being (see fig. 12). One of the contemporary Norwegian architects, Arne Sødal, has followed the inspiration of Knutsen, using the traditional design from the Dragon Style period in a new church in Norway (see figs 13 and 14).

Architecture's role in improving our lives makes it part of a larger setting. This overall setting shows architecture in the light of man's existential situation. Architecture is not only aesthetics; it does also concern human life in general and is in some way connected with philosophy or even metaphysics. It plays its part in shaping man – his consciousness, his relationship to nature and his relationship with society. That is why architecture is not just fun on paper, totally oblivious of any social responsibilities. Architecture as such can heal, but it can also cause illness. It is thus of utmost importance that the architects of to-day can understand this overall setting – both in its human and social context – when carrying out their work. Architecture itself will always be a voice of totality – whether good or bad. It is therefore better to choose the right one instead of not making a choice at all and thereby without realizing it serve a bad, i.e. a negative, totality.

Making architects aware of the totality within which they work within should be an important part of the curriculum when studying architecture. This is about bringing cultural awareness into the study.

References

[1] Bergson, H. 1989, *Essai sur les données immédiates de la conscience,* Paris, Félix Alcan. Translated into English by F. L. Pogson (1910) under the title *Time and free will,* London, G. Allen and Unwin.

[2] Krier, L. 1999, 'Contemporary Perspectives', in Crowe, N., Economakis, R. and Lykoudis, M. (eds) *Building Cities*, London, Artmedia Press.

Traditional Architecture of the Arabian Gulf

Building on Desert Tides

R. HAWKER, *Zayed University, Dubai*

This book chronicles the florescence of architecture in the Arabian Gulf after the expulsion of the Portuguese in the early 1600s. It demonstrates how the power vacuum created by the collapse of Portuguese control over the trade routes in the Indian Ocean encouraged a growth in fortified architecture, especially in Oman, that radiated out to the surrounding region. It also shows how that architecture was slowly replaced by new patterns in domestic and public architecture and town planning throughout the Gulf as trade lines were secured and individual states moved towards new forms of governance.

The book documents the building and crafts of this era and analyses them within the framework of the political, economic, and social information available through primary sources from the period in a way that is both intelligent and accessible. It considers the settlements as part of a larger-connected network of cities, towns and villages and focuses both on how the buildings provided innovative solutions to the demanding climate and yet incorporated new decorative and functional ideas.

Topics are illustrated with photographs of the buildings as they are now, historic photographs from archival and museum collections, line drawings and computer-generated constructions.

The book is therefore attractive to a number of different audiences such as people interested in architectural history, including those who live in or travel to the Gulf as well as people with an interest in Arab and Islamic design, culture and society, vernacular architecture, and post-colonial approaches to colonial history.

ISBN: 978-1-84564-135-1 2008 apx 300pp   apx £89.00/US$178.00/€133.50

WIT PRESS   ...for scientists by scientists

Digital Architecture and Construction

Edited by: A. ALI, University of Seoul, Korea and C.A. BREBBIA, Wessex Institute of Technology, UK

Digital Architecture is a particularly dynamic field that is developing through the work of architecture schools, architects, software developers, researchers, technology, users, and society alike. Featuring papers from the First International Conference on Digital Architecture, this book will be of interest to professional and academic architects involved in the creation of new architectural forms, as well as those colleagues working in the development of new computer codes for engineers, including those working in structural, environmental, aerodynamic fields and others actively supporting advances in digital architecture.

Expert contributions encompass topic areas such as: Database Management Systems for Design and Construction; Design Methods, Processes and Creativity; Digital Design, Representation and Visualization; Form and Fabric; Computer Integrated Construction and Manufacturing; Human–Machine Interaction; Connecting the Physical and the Virtual Worlds; Knowledge Based Design and Generative Systems; Linking Training, Research and Practice; Web Design Analysis; The Digital Studio; Urban Simulation; Virtual Architecture and Virtual Reality; Collaborative Design; Social Aspects.

WIT Transactions on The Built Environment, Vol 90

ISBN: 1-84564-047-0 2006   272pp   £85.00/US$155.00/€127.50

**We are now able to supply you with details of new WIT Press titles via E-Mail. To subscribe to this free service, or for information on any of our titles, please contact the Marketing Department, WIT Press, Ashurst Lodge, Ashurst, Southampton, SO40 7AA, UK
Tel: +44 (0) 238 029 3223
Fax: +44 (0) 238 029 2853
E-mail: marketing@witpress.com**

WITPRESS ...*for scientists by scientists*

The Great Structures in Architecture

From Antiquity to Baroque

F.P. ESCRIG, Universidad de Sevilla, Spain

Starting in antiquity and finishing in the Baroque, this book provides a complete analysis of significant works of architecture from a structural viewpoint. A distinguished architect and academic, the author's highly illustrated exploration will allow readers to better understand the monuments, get closer to them and to explore whether they should be conserved or modified.

Contents: Stones Resting on Empty Space; The Invention of the Dome; The Hanging Dome; The Ribbed Dome; A Planified Revenge – Under the Shadow of Brunelleschi; The Century of the Great Architects; The Omnipresent Sinan; Even Further; Scenographical Architecture of the 18th Century; The Virtual Architecture of the Renaissance and the Baroque.

Series: Advances in Architecture, Vol 22

ISBN: 1-84564-039-X 2006 272pp   £95.00/US$170.00/€142.50

WIT Press is a major publisher of engineering research. The company prides itself on producing books by leading researchers and scientists at the cutting edge of their specialities, thus enabling readers to remain at the forefront of scientific developments. Our list presently includes monographs, edited volumes, books on disk, and software in areas such as: Acoustics, Advanced Computing, Architecture and Structures, Biomedicine, Boundary Elements, Earthquake Engineering, Environmental Engineering, Fluid Mechanics, Fracture Mechanics, Heat Transfer, Marine and Offshore Engineering and Transport Engineering.

WITPRESS   ...for scientists by scientists

Earth Construction Handbook

The Building Material Earth in Modern Architecture

G. MINKE, Director of the Building Research Institute, Kassel University, Germany

*"...a good introduction to earth as a viable building material...well written
and ordered in a way that makes its content accessible to those with limited
scientific and technical knowledge. The reader's understanding of the subject
is supported by the many useful diagrams, tables and photographs."*

JOURNAL ARCHITECTURAL OF CONSERVATION

"...interesting and well constructed."

E-STREAMS

Refined, updated and expanded for English speaking readers from the author's
bestselling Lehmbau-Handbuch (1994), this book is unique in providing a
survey of applications and construction techniques for a material which is
naturally available and easy to use with even basic craft skills, and produces
hardly any environmental waste. The information given can be practically
applied by engineers, architects, builders, planners, craftsmen and laymen
who wish to construct cost-effective buildings which provide a healthy,
balanced indoor climate.

Partial Contents: Properties of Earth as a Building Material; Rammed
Earth Work; Earthblock Work; Large Blocks and Prefabricated Panels; Loam
Plasters; Weather Protection of Loam Surfaces; Repair of Loam Components;
Designs of Particular Building Elements.

Series: Advances in Architecture, Vol 10

ISBN: 1-85312-805-8 2000 216pp b/w diagrams & photographs
£48.00/US$76.00/€72.00